Praise for
Moods of Motherhood

Each page of this book contains another pi
evocatively that speaks to my soul on a lev
at once, her words make me laugh, cry, bre
This book is a gold mine of must-read lov................ .... every mama will
enjoy as well as find truth in it.

Summer Thorp-Lancaster, Summer Doula.com

Lucy's writing is gutsy, honest, touching, and very real. Her words leap off the page to reach right into the heart of the mothering life. She does not shy away from 'ugly' topics and in so doing makes a potent, vibrant, necessary connection to that which we find in ourselves, but may not voice.

Molly Remer, Talk Birth.com; author of *Womanrunes*

Lucy's frank and forthright style paired with beautiful language and her talent for storytelling will have any parent nodding, crying and laughing along – appreciating the good and the bad, the hard and the soft, the light and the dark. It is a must-read for any new mother.

Lucy's column and blog helped me through my own parenting journey, and Moods of Motherhood will be a wonderful companion to the new mother as she finds her own way through the maze of wonderment that comes with becoming a mama. Consider this a tribe of mothers to carry with you wherever you go, so that you can find comfort and companionship at all times – especially when those mothers around you are putting on a brave face!

Zoe Foster, *JUNO* magazine

Lucy's honesty about her life as a full time homemaker, with three children and a multitude of other hats she wears, will take you on a gentle roller coaster ride of emotions!
I laughed and cried all the way through this book, and identified with so much of it! Hugely recommended to all mothers. . . and fathers if you want some insight into our lives!

Rachael Hertogs, author of *Menarche: a journey into womanhood*

So many parenting books out there actually have very little in them about the parents. Lucy on the other hand writes from the heart of the mother to all mothers. She talks of the joys and the love of having children but she also talks of the things unspoken; about anger and guilt. It has been so helpful to me to read of a real mother, so much like me, so much like all of us. Reading this book I feel I am walking along side others, I feel comforted by the fact that I am not alone in my mixture of feelings, my mixture of abilities.
I cannot recommend this book enough!

Laura Angel, Nestled Under Rainbows

Moods of Motherhood took me by surprise – I marvel at how well Lucy has managed to convey the mixed emotional bag that is motherhood. In one entry she captures the sheer joy of watching your children grow and learn, and I think "yes, that's what motherhood is all about" and in the next she writes of the mind-numbing frustration that you can feel, and I nod along and think "Yes, I have been here too."
I loved Lucy's book because it reminded me that we are not alone, that the highs and lows of motherhood are normal, real, and to be embraced.

Lisa Healy, award-winning blogger at Mama.ie

Moods of Motherhood gets under your skin and into your veins – something very few mothering books manage to do. Lucy's raw honesty and fearless approach to expressing all facets of motherhood means that the reader can relax and feel they don't need to be anything other than who they already are.
There's no moral agenda to make you a *nicer* mother, or a *better* one – yet if women follow her advice about looking after their *whole* selves, and in particular, nurturing and tending to their unique creative inner flame, then the consequence of that is no doubt a happier, more balanced mother, and a more contented mother undoubtedly means a ripple effect on her family and home life in general.

Paula Cleary, Go With The Flow Doula.co.uk

Moods
of
Motherhood

the inner journey of mothering

Other books by the same author

*Moon Time : harness the ever-changing energy of your
menstrual cycle*

*The Rainbow Way : cultivating creativity in the midst
of motherhood*

*Reaching for the Moon: A girl's guide to her cycles
(Also available in Polish, Dutch and French editions)*

Burning Woman

Anthology contributor

Earth Pathways Diary 2011–16

Musing on Mothering mothersmilkbooks.com (2012)

Tiny Buddha's Guide to Loving Yourself Hay House (2013)

*Roots: Where Food Comes From and Where It Takes Us:
A Blogher Anthology (2013)*

If Women Rose Rooted Sharon Blackie (2016)

She Rises: Vol. 2 Mago Books (2016)

Also from Womancraft Publishing

The Heart of the Labyrinth – Nicole Schwab

Reaching for the Moon: A girl's guide to her cycles – Lucy H. Pearce

*Moon Time: harness the ever-changing energy of your
menstrual cycle* – Lucy H. Pearce

The Other Side of the River – Eila Kundrie Carrico

The Heroines Club – Melia Keeton-Digby

Burning Woman – Lucy H. Pearce

Liberating Motherhood – Vanessa Olorenshaw

Moon Dreams 2017 Diary – Starr Meneely

Moods
of
Motherhood

the inner journey of mothering

LUCY H. PEARCE

WOMANCRAFT PUBLISHING

Moods of Motherhood: the inner journey of mothering
Copyright 2012: Lucy H. Pearce.
Second edition, Copyright 2014: Lucy H. Pearce.

All rights reserved. No part of this publication may be reproduced, distributed, or transmitted in any form or by any means, including photocopying, recording, or other electronic or mechanical methods, without the prior written permission of the publisher, except in the case of brief quotations embodied in critical reviews and certain other non-commercial uses permitted by copyright law.

Many thanks to *JUNO* magazine for allowing me to reproduce my columns in this book. www.junomagazine.com. Also to *Modern Mum* and *The Mother* magazines and the following anthologies: *Note to Self; Musings on Mothering* and *Roots: A BlogHer anthology* for articles which previously appeared there.

Cover Design: Nick Welsh, Design Deluxe
Typeset by Lucent Word

Published by Womancraft Publishing, 2014
www.womancraftpublishing.com

ISBN: 978-1-910559-21-5

To all the mothers,
the readers of Dreaming Aloud,
online and in *JUNO* magazine,
thank you for your unending support.

Preface to the new edition

Moods of Motherhood was originally written and compiled whilst I was working at the coalface of new motherhood, with three children under five. They were the most intense, challenging, beautiful, endless, love-filled, exhausting years of my life.

This book is a scrapbook of emotions. A journal of the journey through the madness and tenderness of early motherhood. . . and out the other side. In the blur of it all, it is often hard to see and feel the reality of mothering properly, to find the time, let alone the words, to clarify the experience. It is my hope that my own reflections, photographs and musings on the whirlwind of early motherhood can help you to connect to your own inner terrain. . . and value it. Perhaps it will even inspire you to speak or write your own stories and memories.

I am aware that some of the pieces in here may seem extreme. That's because the experience was just that! I described it to people as being tied to the front of a speeding train. I was a young mother, who had three children in four and a half years, whilst trying to establish my own career to help support our young family. We had three highly sensitive kiddies who each woke multiple times a night till they were two. They needed a whole lot more from me than I felt I had to give. I was trying to be a good attachment parent – and struggling with my failings. I didn't know it at the time but I had adrenal burnout. Pregnancy depression. And post-partum depression. It is no exaggeration to say that writing saved me.

And it seems that this raw honesty about my own experience is what connected so deeply with my readers. Women who had never dared speak aloud about the hidden sides of motherhood saw themselves in my book. And they reached out. Many times I was thanked for saving another mother's life. For speaking the words that were in her heart.

That is not something I take lightly.

Mothering is the work of the heart, soul and body. And yet our culture has no interest in how it feels to do it. Nor in the effects it has on us. All that is required is that we choose the right diapers and sleep routines, and have quiet children who say please and thank you. And smile and be grateful. The inner world of the mother, who creates the climate within which our families, and communities grow, is almost entirely overlooked and undervalued.

The basic premise seems to be: mothering doesn't matter. It's not real work, so be grateful, shut up and don't complain. If you're not finding that it all comes naturally, if it's not all delightful, then you are a bad mother and therefore don't deserve to have kids.

Shame ranks highly in the arsenal of weapons to keep mothers compliant and submissive. As does comparison to other successful paragons of mothering virtue. Women's work has never been properly valued in our culture. In part because women have been second class citizens for so long. In part because women's bodies and inner realities are not understood. And in part because it is done in private: within our bodies and our homes. We gestate our babies unseen. Rock and nurse them alone at home. Survive dinner time. Worry about finances. Try to reclaim flagging libidos. Curse stretchmarks and wobbly bits. Angst over school choices. Smart at criticisms of our parenting. . . in private.

I soon realized what an epidemic there is of under-supported, overstretched mothers. Working their own personal coalface every day. Women who love their children, and yet struggle with the daily mothering grind. Women who are struggling with mental health issues, often undiagnosed or poorly treated.

Suffering from extreme sleep deprivation. Lack of support – be it financial, cultural and emotional. Women who feel very alone. . . whilst doing the hardest job in the world. Wondering if they are doing OK. Wishing they were doing better. Scared to say anything in case they are judged incompetent and incapable, and the source of their anguish – but also their deepest love – their precious children – are plucked from their less than perfect hands.

And so women struggle on in silence. Knowing that they, or the reality they are experiencing, must be wrong. . . because it doesn't match up to everything they are told about the truth of motherhood, that soft-focus, unending love, joy and delight – by the authorities: the baby books, experts, public health nurses, doctors and movies.

This book is a celebration and acknowledgement of *all* the moods of motherhood. Not just the pretty, nice, acceptable ones. But the dark, murky, unspoken, unspeakable, confusing, ambiguous ones too. All of these and more are tangled together to make up the tapestry of our mothering days.

Readers commend me for my honesty and raw emotion. For my willingness to tell it how it is. Whilst I try to write exclusively about my own inner experience of mothering, I am very mindful that it is never just my life I am writing about, but that of my partner, children and community too.

What concerns me is whether in future they will read something which they wished they did not know. My hope is that they will get a more rounded understanding of me, their mother, my frailties and my glories. An insight into the real inner life of women and mothers everywhere, which is usually papered over or sugar-coated. Time will tell. But I hope they never feel that their lives and privacy have been exploited. We are, in the end, all connected, and writing about my personal mothering journey brings them along for the ride. For that I am very grateful.

Speaking the truth of our experiences of motherhood can place us in a very vulnerable position. To speak what is normally kept hidden and silent can open us to judgment and criticism. It can give people permission to unleash their hidden inner conflicts, self-judgments, personal suffering and doubts on us. To mistake our failings for theirs. I know, I have experienced it myself. And watched many other women – brave, courageous, raw, loving, imperfect, sensitive women – experience this too. It is endemic in a culture which hides away its dark sides, and allows only the positive.

I see now that words are our greatest power. Being able to take the amorphous tangle of contradictory feelings and speak them out, write them out – make sense of them for ourselves and share them with others. This is how we not only survive, but thrive, in this unfamiliar land of motherhood. And we thrive best if we share our stories, if we find support in others.

Here's to your flourishing. That you will learn from all the myriad moods of motherhood. That you and your children will thrive as you grow together and find shared language and love in your experiences and memories.

Lucy H. Pearce, Shanagarry, 2014.

A note on layout

The majority of these posts were written for online readers – a different style of writing and layout to your average book. Blog writing favors short punchy sentences, shorter pieces of work, and white space between the paragraphs. I have decided to retain this style throughout the book.

Contents

Preface to the new edition ix

Introduction 1

Being a mother 5

    Nobody told me. . . 6

    Doing it right –
        what I knew before having kids 6

    Mother blessing 11

    Note to self 13

    The myth of happy families why it just can't work,
        and how you're doing just fine 15

    Mama bear 17

    Reflection of a mother 18

    My four children 19

    Tribal parenting – the sustainable model 21

    Mother tongue:
        creating a positive language of mothering 24

    The sacred role of a parent 26

    The mother-soul 29

    Speaking for birth 32

    Pain 35

    Layer cake 36

Tenderness 39

    Bye bye baby 40

    Breastfeeding 41

    The lost art of lullaby 43

    Sweeter with you 46

    The memory keeper 48

Ambiguity   **51**

The waves and the shore   52

Holding tight. . . letting go   53

The blur   55

happy days   56

Depression   **59**

The baby blues   60

Failure   62

Not Normal
(otherwise known as mothering with mental illness)   63

Why getting back to normal is the biggest mistake
you can make   70

Joy   **73**

Joy pockets   74

The taste of cherry blossom   74

An Eden to call our own   77

Candlelight, fairylight, firelight   78

So glad I'm here!   80

Guilt   **83**

Getting over guilt   84

The perfect mother   86

Caring   **89**

Welcome to the circle   90

How do you treat yourself?   92

Creativity   **97**

Creative renaissance and the womb   98

Dancing   103

Sleep   **105**

Adventures without sleep   106

Routine and rhythm   109

Shared sleep   112

Are you a morning goddess? 113

I don't want to go to bed 114

Embracing change 117

In transition 118

Milestones 120

Learning to fly 122

Baby steps and belief 124

Love 127

More than the whole world 128

The matador 128

Tender 129

What's love got to do with it? 130

The power of love 133

Competitiveness 135

An end to mama bashing 136

Time poverty and the modern mum 138

Stop with the sunshine! 141

Super woman and the good enough mum 143

happy days 145

Pride 147

I see you baby! 148

Finding our balance 149

Anger and fierceness 151

The tiger mother: guardian of boundaries 152

The white heat of mama anger 154

Is the silencing of mama anger a feminist issue? 158

The confessions of a domesticated wild woman 159

Mama's home 161

Growling at our mothers 163

Mindful mama moon time 165

Grief   **167**

The grieving mother soul   168

Almost   169

Patience   **171**

I quit!   172

Let's play!   172

The doula   174

Learning   **175**

Emotional stew with dumplings on top   176

On starting school   177

Damn you compulsory education!   178

Summer holidays – sibling revelry   180

happy days   182

Highly sensitive   **185**

The watchful Buddha boy   186

I can't cope – dealing with overwhelm   188

Home making   **193**

There's no place like home   194

The non-domestic goddess shines her sink   195

Radical Homemakers:
  of housewives and feminists   197

Spring clearing   201

Cooking with love   202

Christmas is coming and mama's getting panicked   204

A mothering badge of honor for a day well done   206

Playful   **209**

I am an idiot   210

Jesus in a space ship
  (the zany world of a five-year-old boy)   210

The Game of Life   212

A mother's prayer   215

About the author   **216**

Introduction

When I was the mother of one, I thought I was an expert. Which is why I became a writer on parenting issues! As the mother of three, I have been humbled to my core. I have realized just how much I don't know or can't do – and just how little I am 'in control'. And yet ironically with that knowledge and acceptance, comes a little more wisdom, and a lot more experience.

This book is far from a parenting manual written by an objective expert. Rather it is the life of a mother – warts and all. It is compiled from posts written for my blog, *Dreaming Aloud*, published articles and previously unpublished work. So here, for you, is a journey through the emotional terrain of a mother, from humor to heartbreak, though the story is mine, it could be yours.

I see new friends starting out on the road to motherhood with mixed feelings. Immense joy at the ecstasy of love they are about to experience, great protectiveness, wishing to shield them from the scars it will make on their souls, the pain, the heartache, the worry, the exhaustion, and the anger which they may have been able to keep hidden all these years. But this is the journey. The one that makes us the mothers that we will be. The mothers that our children will live with every day, yet barely know.

Becoming a mother brings with it such a vast raft of complications for the psyche, before you add the momentous task of caring for a small and ever-changing child to the mix. Becoming a mother reawakens our own feelings, good and bad, about our own mothers. It changes our relationship with our partner forever: suddenly we are not just lovers but parents. And it shifts us instantaneously into the next generation, causing potentially seismic shifts in friendships where one set are not parents and we now are. Not to mention the adjustment between us and our families of origin. And that is before we even consider the massive shift in roles for most modern women from full time work or study out in the world, to suddenly being at home, if only for the first weeks, with a small being who needs you all the time. Ideas of women's roles in society suddenly become less abstract or idealized, and the whole dilemma of who cares for the child, who works, who pays the bills and how suddenly become pressing realities with few ideal answers.

My grandmother always said, "You are your baby's weather." How true that is! There is nothing more remarkable about the act of mothering than the changing moods. The weather of motherhood can seemingly alter from moment to moment, day to day, a rollercoaster of emotions stronger than one has ever experienced before. The stakes, after all, are far higher than anything we have ever played for before: the very life, health and happiness of a creature that is our own flesh and blood.

On reading back over my blog, I noticed how contrasting posts follow one day after the other – all so real, yet so intangible. Like the weather we are only left with vague memories and snapshots of how hot or cold it was, no real yardstick of the tempests and sunshine of our mothering years.

Thousands of mothers around the world were drawn to these posts, these outpourings of emotion, frustration, joy and despondency. It seems we are all yearning for a reflection of our own tumultuous experiences, a validation of the endless emotional turmoil and physical exhaustion which motherhood reeks in our lives. We seem to lack a language to share both the mundane repetitiveness of our daily mothering lives, as well as a forum for sharing the deeper emotional parts. For perhaps the first time in history, the mothers of the twentieth and twenty first centuries mothered alone, in separate houses, often far from family support. The job of parenting is not meant to be handled by one adult, it takes a tribe.

Few of us entered the role prepared, though we might have been expecting (some) sleepless nights and smelly nappies, the all-consuming nature of motherhood lay hidden, until we were well and truly embarked on our maiden voyage. The sweetness of a first baby's smile did not reveal the cacophony of demands which another child – or three – would bring.

Most knew how they wanted to be, and what they most certainly would not do. And then after the first glow of motherhood had worn off, the disappointments begin stacking up: the ideals which had fallen by the wayside, the perfection not achieved, due to lack of energy, experience, insight or something else.

And at that point we can despair and see ourselves as failing. But the mothering journey does not, cannot, stop that day; even though we feel we cannot continue. And it is in overcoming these moments that we find ourselves as the mothers we truly are. In these moments we have to let the perfect mother die, and embrace our quirky, impatient, silly, messy, deeply loving mother selves.

Very often I find it hard to be really mentally present with my children – though I aspire to be. I find the demands of motherhood too intense, their needs too much. And so I do what I know, what I love: I write. In writing I capture the mood, the moment in a more effective way than my whirling thoughts and fuzzy memory could ever hope to. And so I find that even in my moments of despair, distraction and elation I was present. And in these vignettes of mothering life, and the images which accompany them, I have captured the whole process of motherhood which was at times almost unbearable in the actual living of it.

And so I have it here in all its preciousness to savor, and give thanks for, from the safe distance of time and the security of the written word. Yet, as I read back, I realize with great poignancy that these babies that I was capturing have grown, almost without me noticing, despite my almost daily writing about them. They are bigger and stronger, little rugged human beings out in the world. Little humans that I co-created, that I carried in my belly and fed from my breast – the eldest is now up to my shoulder. His feet only three sizes smaller than mine! I feel like I need to pinch myself, it doesn't seem real, or even possible. And yet it is. And that is the miracle of motherhood.

I feel duty bound to tell you that it has gotten easier as they – and we – have grown in understanding of ourselves and each other. As they – and we – have found language to communicate our needs, desires and peculiarities. And as they have become school age. I have found my balance as a creative professional and mother. We have found our feet as a family. Our life is full. Challenging. But it is ours. Our family has been co-created in our own image. Holding each of us in our unique strengths and vulnerabilities. And for that I am very grateful.

I look forward to sharing my journey with you and hope that it might give you insight and support in your own life as a mother.

Being a mother

What does it mean to be a mother?

It is more than a name. More than a job. More than a role.

It is an art form. A meditative practice in the school of life.

It is a life's work which changes you on every level, almost every day of your life.

Once the spark of motherhood is lit in your soul, no matter how long your children are with you, it never goes out.

Nobody told me. . .

You look at me bewildered, eyes gray with exhaustion. Milk-spattered, baggy clothes, hair awry.

"Nobody told me. . ." you begin.

You look at me, urging me to explain myself. How could I have kept this, all of this, secret from you? Surely it was my duty to prepare you.

"Nobody told me how much it would hurt, how exhausted I would feel, how much love I have in my heart that I think I will burst, how overwhelming it all is. . ." her eyes begin to well with the enormity of her new knowing.

All I can do is to smile. To hold her.

"We tried," I say softly. Stroking her tousled hair.

And I think to myself. It is not so much that we did not tell you, as you could not hear. Until you have your own child, held in your heart, your ears are blocked, your eyes are blind to the reality of motherhood: its pains and its glories. Once you have been there, stood in the body of motherhood, then you can hold hands with every woman who has ever mothered. You know her joys and pains. You are her.

Doing it right – what I knew before having kids

Before I had children I knew, to the marrow of my bones, that I would do it right.

I was born to be a good mother.

A mother who was available, devoted and loving.

A mother who was always there, without question.

I would know how to soothe a crying baby. Though of course my babies would not cry very much.

And my babies would sleep.

Because I would do it right.

And my children would be kind, loving and well-behaved.

Interesting, popular and creative.

And they would get on – no sibling rivalry here.

Because I would do it right.

There was so much I would teach them.

I would pour every ounce of my hard-won wisdom and knowledge into them so that they could take the high road to enlightenment.

I had a lot of confidence in myself. And my power to make everything right.

This is the (unspoken) core belief of most yet-to-be parents: if I am a good person – which I am – then it will all be fine. Because I will be in control of it all. I WILL DO IT RIGHT.

And then pregnancy came.

And there were so many choices.

And so many variables outside of my control.

And it wasn't just my opinions to consider but my husband's . . .

And my parents'.

And his parents'.

And my university's.

And his boss'.

And the doctors'.

And the three different midwives'.

And they all thought we should be sure to do it right.

But each of their 'rights' looked very, very different.

For one it was multiple scans. For another the bare minimum.

For one it was home birth, for many others it was hospital birth or sure death . . .

And then my son was born.

And for a moment it was perfect.

Until he couldn't latch on properly.

And my preconceived plan of doing it right was shot through.

I always knew I would breastfeed.

Exclusively.

And we tried and we tried.

And I cried and cried.

But on the second night I sent my husband out for formula.

Because 'right' was keeping our child alive. Not values.

I nearly lost my doula friend forever over that.

I didn't use the formula that night.

Or the next.

But already I had been humbled.

I now knew that I did not know. That I wasn't in control.

That doing it right was not an easy path. Or a clear one.

I realized that in someone's eyes I'd always be doing it wrong . . .

Even sometimes in my own.

My children were born with their own unique personalities.

For some reason they did not (always!) think I was the font of all wisdom.

Actually they wanted to do it their way.

And make mistakes.

And fall . . . even out of windows.

Even if I wanted to make sure they were always safe. I couldn't.

They came in with their own unique anxieties that I couldn't reason away.

And their own visions about what constituted 'a good night's sleep'.

And just how attached they felt they needed to be.

And the storm winds of post-natal depression rocked my boughs and threatened to uproot me.

I wasn't the happy, doting perfect stay-at-home mother I was supposed to be.

I was impatient, bored and frustrated . . .

During the early years of motherhood I learned so much, so fast . . .

I learned that I'm not in control of many of the things I wished I was.

And that I'm responsible for lots of things I wish I wasn't.

I learned that books do not have all the answers. Nobody does.

And that the important work goes on unnoticed, unheralded, in the midst of boring Sunday afternoons, and the early hours of Tuesday mornings or trips to the hospital. This is when my wisdom, my influence is imparted. When it is stripped of any sort of mama-propaganda and carefully-constructed wise lessons.

They learn from the fullness of me – my strengths (often ones I never thought were very important) and my weaknesses (things that I was previously able to whitewash out of my self-image).

I learned that society expects me to be perfect – but will be damned if it's going to help or support me, even by widening doorways so my pram can fit in.

And I realized that the only game in town is the game of judging other parents and believing we could do it better.

Experts do it.

The government and health and education authorities do it.

The older generations do it.

Other parents do it.

Childless people do it.

The media whips up frenzies about it.

Sometimes we laugh at the stupidity of parents who should know better.

And sometimes we are outraged.

As though there were some perfect way. And the irresponsible individual just needs to learn better to do it right.

I still catch myself doing it sometimes. (Though I have gotten better.)

And I'm sure you do it too. Sometimes. (Maybe?)

But at least it is now tempered with the knowledge of just how hard a job it is. And how many variables there are.

And how little we are really in control.

And just how different each family, each individual child is.

And that there really is no one 'right way'.

So when a childless friend lets drop that I should do this or that.

Or that they would NEVER do it that way.

I give the patient look, and laugh quietly inside, knowing, that one day too, they will taste their own judgment, will sense their own powerless in the midst of the most important work of their life.

And they will remember their certainty with bashfulness.

And then they, too, will judge a little less.

And I will love them twice as much when they are struggling.

Because now they know, too.

There is no 'right way'.

And none of us, not even our children, are perfect.

We are all doing what we can, with what we have, where we are.

And that is good enough. . . because it's all we have.

This post was written for inclusion in the monthly Carnival of Natural Parenting, on the theme – "Parenting in Theory vs. in Reality" hosted by Code Name: Mama and Hobo Mama. It was the featured post on the Natural Parents' Network.

Mother blessing

We live in a baby-centric world which is delighted to pat your belly and coo over your baby.

We offer baby showers to shower the glowing mama-to-be with gifts of nappy cakes and baby bouncers, vests and toys. But somewhere, in the midst of it all, something rather important is often lost. . .

That's right: the mama.

We ask, "How's the baby? What's the baby up to? When are you due?"

But not the most important question of all, "How are *you*?"

How are you mama? In the complexity of it all, can you share your longing, your worries, your hopes, your boredom, your excitement, your multiple discomforts, the love which pierces your heart and makes it feel it might explode, your bone shattering exhaustion, your need to be held and cared for, and your tigress desire to be left alone?

In our community of women, we offer something different to the traditional baby shower: a mother blessing. Something which is dedicated to caring for you. Nourishing you. Holding you. Loving you. Listening to you.

A sacred circle surrounding you. Sharing our wisdom. Hearing your fears. Massaging your hands, soaking your feet, painting henna on your belly, brushing your hair, lighting a candle for you, wishing you blessings on your birth and new child. Sometimes we string a necklace with wishes or birth stories, we burn fears on the fire, and other times we make a belly cast and paint it, or trace clay labyrinths with our fingers. And finally feasting with you and filling your fridge and freezer with nourishment for the weeks ahead.

This I offer you here. And I light a candle for you.

Blessings on our children, for they have a long way to go,

Blessings on our elders, for they have travelled far.

And blessings on those of us in between, for we are doing the work.

Please accept this virtual mother blessing to nourish your body and soul, which never for a second stops nourishing that precious life within.

May it sustain you during the birth, and in the days and weeks afterwards.

May you learn the art of surrendering with grace. May you be humbled in the face of your immense power. May your heart be broken open with tenderness. May you be held up on wings of love.

Blessings on you, dearest mama.

Note to self

Dearest mama,

You started out with such high hopes, big dreams – how you would help the world to embrace your dear sweet children. You whispered your promises to them in the womb. Of how you would be the perfect mother – ever gentle, kind and patient. Of how you would do everything for them, with them. And you truly meant it.

For years you tried to be the perfect mama. But the pain that you weren't was almost unbearable. You felt a failure. You felt guilty. You felt like giving up, running away. Often you threatened to quit.

Don't be hard on yourself. You are the only mama they know. The only mama they love. The only mama you know how to be. And that is more than enough.

You wanted to make your past better through your mothering. But you can't. You can't erase your own pain, however hard you try to be perfect or love your children more.

You do your best not to recreate your own suffering in their lives. You are committed to love. You are conscientious. And that has to be enough. The world does not change in a day, and neither will you. Remember you are your ancestors' hopes and dreams incarnate. But you are also their hurts and failings writ large.

You love your children, though you may shout at them. You feed them and put up with their complaints when they don't like dinner. You clothe them and weather their tantrums over too-tight clothes. You mother them at six in the morning, at lunchtime, at midnight when they wake with sore teeth. When you are sick, you mother them still. You tend to their hurt knees with a mother's love. You help them to find the answers their souls are seeking. You tickle and tumble with them. You show them the size of a mother's love and the reality of a mother's life. You give them language with which to engage with the world. You hold their hearts in your hand and ask them about their dreams. You throw your sticks together into the river of life. Now watch them float. You are not meant to be their pilot. Let go with the flow. Let it wash over you all.

You spend so long focusing on the minutiae – the moments that you yell, not the moments that you embrace them, which in the bigger picture far out-number the cross words and impatience which you feel colors your days.

You can be sure that what they will hold in their souls are all the things you cannot see – the way your hair falls over your face as you kiss them goodnight, the soft pillow of breast as they snuggle up to you, the way you say certain words, the magical contents of your jewelry box, your love of books, the way you loved them when they felt ill and frightened. When you cheered loudly for them in the school play or showed your heartfelt appreciation of their creations. And fleeting moments when you stood hand in hand on the edge of the ocean in the light of the full moon.

Just try, for a moment to see yourself through their eyes. See yourself as the most important woman in their world.

Because that is what you are. You, dearest woman, are a goddess to them, though they will never tell you. You are love incarnate. Your perceived flaws just make you human.

Allow yourself to feel the depth and breadth of your love. Their love. Nothing else matters.

Lucy x

This is my contribution to Note to Self: The Secret to Becoming your own Best Friend by Jo MacDonald.

The myth of happy families why it just can't work, and how you're doing just fine

How's your day?

Chances are you're tired. Or beating yourself up at getting cross with a child. Or have just had to break up a fight. Or are hiding on the internet just to get five minutes peace.

Or perhaps you are feeling very chuffed because for the last half an hour everything has gone perfectly. You are, for the moment anyway, living the dream. You *are* the perfect parent.

But then the baby will start screaming uncontrollably. . . the older kids will start yelling. . . you will long for a moment's peace. . . and, if you're anything like me, you'll feel like a failure, again.

As a mother your job is to be the creator and sustainer of love, peace and harmony. At all times. Anything less and you've failed. Especially if the outburst is coming from *you* at the end of your tether. (I may, perhaps, be speaking from experience here!)

The biggest myth about having kids, is that every day is supposed to be saccharine happy, with everyone in perfect harmony. And that it is your moral responsibility.

STOP THE LIGHTS and BREATHE!

The best thing you can do for your sanity, is stop believing this rubbish! It's only taken me 8 1/2 years to realize this! So if you're just starting out, go easy on yourself!

We were standing in the kitchen this morning, my husband was feeling despondent because our girls were being cranky with him, I was being cranky with him, the kids were bickering on the sofa. . . and had been since the moment they woke up.

A sudden realization hit me: this is how it is 70% of the time. . .

Someone in the family is out of sorts about something. Yet we spend our whole time denying this, resisting it, getting angry about it: thinking it should all be roses and hearts, holding hands and walking into the sunshine. Because that's the way were told it should be.

All the movies show it. All books show it. Permanently smiling children. Permanently smiling parents.

We know they're fiction – but some part of our souls holds it as incontrovertible truth, and holds us ransom to it.

Sure we can do it in the outside world. We do with our friends, they do it with their friends. We're pretty good at playing happy families on best behavior.

But then the door closes. And here we are, together again, in private with the housework and homework, tired, hungry, overwhelmed, wanting space, frustrated, bored, sick. . .

Home is where we do real life. Home is where we get to be real people. Where we let out our unshowable parts and get to be antisocial when we are sick, feeling alone, tired, when the weather's bad, when life's just kicked us hard between the teeth, when our hearts are breaking or depression pulls us down. This is where we get to be unvarnished, verrucas, stretch marks and all.

And a lot of the time it aint pretty. At least not in the way we are taught pretty *should* be. . . But it is pretty real.

This is where we get to grow. Home is our growing edge, our creative crucible of soul.

Our perfect vision of how parenting will be, should be, is a cardboard cut-out. It doesn't leave any room for human mess: surfaces covered in junk, unwashed dishes, peed on sheets, engorged breasts and milk stained tops, bickering over who got the least sleep, the sour milk in your coffee, baby waking up just as you manage to get into the shower. . . after hours of waiting.

In a movie it's funny, we see the ridiculous side of it. But in real life, it often feels rather depressing. We want to be living in Technicolor: the kisses without the tears; the cute paintings without all the mess; the well-fed baby without the puke; the sleeping angel, without the nightmares.

What we want is the life that we see in the perfect family portrait: well lit, clean faces and clothes, everyone smiling, hanging on the sitting room wall with pride. We define ourselves by this. This is who we *really* are, we tell ourselves. The rest is just a mistake, an inconvenience, a failure. We conveniently edit it from our memories, write it off as 'not really us'.

But what if the crankiness, mayhem, madness, mess, mishaps and tears are an integral a part of the process that creates that magical moment which we capture and frame? They are us too. Life is the creative process, the endless churning and changing of a family in flux, individuals like atoms spinning here and there, only for a moment vibrating at the same frequency. It takes just one to shift slightly and we have dissonance again. Dissonance, not harmony, is the normal state of affairs. . . though our peace loving hippy selves wish otherwise.

Family living is the ultimate creativity. There will be paint on the table, puke on your shoulder, poop on your fingers. . . And possibly the bottom of your shoe! Tears and tantrums are all part of the process. From all of us! This messiness behind the scenes is like the artist at work, creating the most beautiful work of art: a human family.

Mama bear

I am your mama bear. And you are my cub. Forever and ever I love you. . .

I will growl at the badness in the world, and keep you safe from harm. . . but I will not do everything for you or wrap you in cotton wool.

I will feed your belly, but I will not make you endless snacks that lie half-eaten.

I will snuggle you to sleep, but I will not lie like a sucker whilst you play for hours.

I will breastfeed you, but growl if you nip or tie me down all day.

I will teach you all I know, but I will not do your homework for you.

I will kiss your hurts, but also let you feel your own pain.

I am a mama bear, and I have my own wildness. I must hunt and prowl myself.

And you must too.

We are wild ones you and I. Let us not domesticate each other too much. Do not tie me in bondage and I will let your heart roam free too.

Reflection of a mother

I see a mother in a big cozy bed, her little ones clambering over her like puppies, all tousle-haired from sleep. What a pretty picture of family life.

I see the mother. But I do not see her as she is. I see the teenager with forty pounds and a double chin added. Oh, how she hates that double chin. It is all she sees in every picture of mothering bliss: the sharp jaw line of youth lost to cake and age. And a gray streak in the hair, how she struggles with the social meaning of that streak. But not the soul meaning: it is moonlight, silver star shine, a blessing brought early by age and wisdom. Why does everyone else hide theirs and pretend they are still 21? What was so great about 21 anyway? The anticipation, the insecurity of youth, embarking on a journey, unbridled and unclear as to her destination or even who is sailing the ship of her body and soul.

She sees the weight around the face, the circles under the eyes that sing of her lack of sleep. Her belly is covered in silver gray lines: ley lines, love lines that heralded hidden mysteries beneath the barrow mound. The fertile hillocks of belly and breast, once full and round, now deflated balloons, sad at the loss of their precious cargo.

When out with these children she thinks she is only a couple of years older than the ten-year-olds she passes kicking a ball on the grass. They must not know that these are her children. They must think she is the babysitter. Her own primary school years were but a heartbeat away to her, not two decades or more.

She cannot see the mother that she is. She sees pictures of her holding her children, but she cannot see what she feels in her bones, the cellular changes which motherhood has wrought on her body and soul. They are invisible in her mirror image. She looks no longer like herself, but she does not look like she feels. Who is this mother, this person in the mirror? It is not me, is it?

My four children

I always thought I would have four children.

Or rather I knew it.

According to my step mother, as a little girl I spoke about it a lot.

My husband and I spoke about it.

Pregnant with my second child I had a dream of four sandcastles on the beach – they were my four children.

After having my third, and my husband's swift vasectomy I felt bereft, distraught, like a piece of the puzzle was missing, forever, there was a rip in the fabric of how my life was intended to be.

And yet I knew I could not care for another child.

When my last child was about six months old I had another dream of four children. And this time my soul sister's only child was my fourth. That felt right. About two days later, unprompted our three-year-old referred to him as "our brother". Interesting.

And then, as you know, I have been wrestling with my need to mother and my need to write.

And it suddenly came to me. I have always referred to my books as my "other children". Only half-jokingly. It is sad. . . but true. My books, whilst all replaceable, hold a map to my soul and growth as a person on every level. And in the past few days it has become clear to me that my 'mission' as a writer is to write the books I have always wanted to read, but never found. My writing is my fourth child.

Just like we can sense our children years before they come to us, so I can with my writing. It takes the love and space and time and patience of a child in my life. It takes my energy and vision. It has my complete devotion and heart – and sometimes it disappoints me.

I am never as good a writer as I want to be. Just like being a mother.

When my first book arrived through the post this week, it truly felt like being a new mama again. The sheer elation, the sense of achievement. The sense of vision, destiny and reality coinciding in one barely believable moment which I had dreamed of all my life, yet did not dare to believe could come true.

I am a newborn mama. I cradle my baby gently, carry her with me everywhere I go. She is precious. Perfect in my eyes. I am beaming with delight, showing her off to everyone: look what I made!

Tribal parenting – the sustainable model

I seem, with increasing frequency, to be having the same conversation with parents. And it goes something like this. . . We love our children, love being their parents, but parenting solo is hard. We value our children being home in their early years. . . but we're struggling with the reality: feeling overwhelmed, isolated, burnt out, frustrated at the repetitive mundanity of domesticity. We love our time parenting together with our spouses, relations and friends, when there are more than one pair of hands and one brain to cope with both children and the domestic tasks that call on us. But alone we struggle. We feel overwhelmed.

There are some that like to knock today's generation of parents as too soft, highlighting how they, or their mother, did it all singlehanded for ten children, during the war, surviving only on ground parsnips, washing laundry by hand in the leach-infested river, from which they carried water five miles home, whilst holding down a part-time job in a sweatshop. I am sure there were many. And still are, all around the world. That, for me, is survival parenting. You do it because you have to, because there are no choices. You get through it the best you can. And if everyone lives, you have managed it.

I am not talking about survival parenting. But optimal, thriving, sustainable parenting. Parenting which nourishes, rather than depletes, parent and child, not to mention the environment. We, and our children are wired for parenting together – and living in extended groups – it is not parenting that is overwhelming – but parenting alone.

For some parenting solo is almost endless – because of separation, a partner working away, or being deceased. For others of us it may be something we do for only hours at a time. The extension of parent's roles, child development, attachment and the sheer speed and complexity of modern life have added hugely to the expectations placed on both parents and children. We are tribal people living in an atomistic world.

In her presentation at the *Light on Parenting* conference, author of *The Science of Parenting*, Margot Sunderland noted wryly that a preschool aged child has a need every 15 seconds. Robin Grille, Australian psychologist and parenting educator, who I interviewed for the summer issue of *JUNO*, said that: "That is one of the reasons why parents and mothers in particular, are very sensitive to guilt, because they're trying to do something that requires a group of people to do. In reality a child requires more than what one parent can offer. A child needs the attention of at least four adults. The human being is designed to live in a cooperative situation. In that situation whenever mum is tired, there is always another pair of hands to take over."

Having lived in a variety of situations whilst being the mother of young children, from living permanently with in-laws, to living in a type of intentional community, and living in a house as a nuclear family, I know from first-hand experience how over-whelmed I, and my children get, when it is just me and them.

I have had a number of moments over the past month that have highlighted the naturalness of tribal parenting simply because they felt so happy and right for all of us. One was when three of us mothers sat round the table to roll Chinese steamed pancakes together – a job I had done a couple of weeks previously, alone in charge of three children. The experiences were so different. The first time round, I felt stressed and the children were bickering. The second time round the children were playing outside together with their friends, and the mothers were talking and rolling round the kitchen table, the work going so much faster with three pairs of hands, At different times a child or two, out of the seven we have between us, would come in, help for a while and drift off again. No stress or strain on anyone, just the pleasure of making food and spending time together.

Another realization was after a blissful two week holiday with my husband and children, first with my in-laws and then a friend. Very rarely in that two weeks was I responsible for all three children and the domestic tasks single-handed. Instead the grouping shifted and morphed through the day – but there was almost always one or more adults around, whilst others were resting, doing domestic work or out alone. Returning home to a house and three children to myself again was a shock to the system which totally freaked me out and overwhelm hit in fast. I felt trapped by my family and my four walls.

I am not trying to marginalize the issues that come with tribalism and extended families – when we live in nuclear families, we have the benefits of privacy and space. We choose how to define our own values and where in the world we live. We are able to be more fully ourselves as individuals. But I am aware of what is lost too. . . and how much more work it is to live separately. How much less sustainable – both with our own energy, and in terms of resources and materials.

Most of the time it feels like there is not enough of us to be all we are supposed to. And so, parent by parent, we are finding our own ways to sustainability. Family by family. We are finding ways to be together, ways to share – cars, home, labor, resources, time together. . . Finding ways to downsize – our possessions, the size of the space we are responsible for, the demands on our time. Finding ways to balance our need for independence and individuality, with our need for a tribe. Little ways and big ways to be healthier, sustainable families.

This was my Dreaming Aloud column in JUNO magazine, Autumn 2013.

Mother tongue: creating a positive language of mothering

"We live in an articulate society, continually questioning ourselves and each other. It is not fair to leave a new mother with a horrific collection of words to condemn her – and almost nothing in the way of praise for when she is doing something well. A whole vocabulary is missing."

What Mothers Do, Naomi Stadlen

I want to share with you some of the positive words I have added to my mothering vocabulary over the past couple of years so that I have a way of talking about – and valuing – the mothering work I do.

A mama – I am most definitely a mama: any female through the act of giving birth or adoption becomes a mother. Mummy is my mother, and it has the connotations for me of poshness and childishness. I am not a mom (American) or mam (Irish), or mum (standard English) All of them are short, curt sounding and conventional. There is no roundness, warmness to those words.

No, I am a mama – soft to cuddle, with big snuggly milk giving boobs and rounded baby carrying hips, honed to soft perfection by our nearly daily family cookie baking and eating. I am a hippy mama, with floaty skirts, to skim over those big hips. I am a sling-wearing, sore knee kissing, jumping on the trampoline together, Arnica prescribing, walking in the woods, roast chicken serving, lullaby singing, candle lighting, playgroup starting, nature table tending, crafty mama.

Mama can be a verb too. Come round my house, any day or night and you will find me mama-ing my little brood. Sometimes with joy and laughter and songs, making play dough and dancing to folk music in the sitting room. And sometimes shouting and screaming and crying and despairing over toddler tantrums, maternal exhaustion from a night waking baby and my need to run away to the other side of the world, now!

An inherent part of mama-ing is **snuggle-time** – a warm, cuddly, lovely time to sink your nose into your child's hair, and give them your warmest most golden sustaining mama-energy, and suck up their sweetness and wish you could bottle it. "Mama snuggle me up" pleads my two-year-old when she is feeling sad or tired. Snuggle time with all my children started with the warm reciprocated joy of liquid love: breastfeeding. As they have got older and weaned, it continues to be a golden time for us.

Breathing is another key mama skill. I find breathing gets me out of a lot of hairy situations. Sometimes breathing is all I can do to stop my mama head from spinning off in sheer frustration. And sometimes I think: *sod breathing I need to shout!* And then I feel very, very guilty.

So **peace-making** is another key mama skill. Making peace with myself for failing myself and my children. Making peace with my children for being a horrible shouty, cranky mama. Making peace between my children when they are tormenting each other. This mama skill is why I think there should be more mamas in 'big' power, out in the world.

Soothing is a variation on snuggle time, but is needed for scared, hurt, shocked children. I picture my Madonna's cloak, and imagine it wrapped around me and my little one, as I rock, cradle and stroke them wherever we may be: shopping center, birthday party, bus or home.

Strewing is another key skill for wanna-be home educators, and hands-on parents. It is the act of scattering carefully thought out ideas, objects, games, books in your child's path, and then jumping out of the way to let them pick it up and take an interest in it, to ask questions in their own time, rather than foisting a 'learning experience' on them.

Day surfing is the act of filling a day with no money, and no plans, seeing where you wash up: head into town, start at the library, then onto the pet shop, watch the road construction team working, a run in the park, listen to a busker. Day surfing is a much larger challenge at home, where it can often be white knuckle survival.

I am sure I will add to this. I invite you to find words for positive acts of mothering. Add to our communal vocabulary, and honor the often challenging, sometimes rewarding, but crucially important act of mothering.

The sacred role of a parent

A lot of the time I worry: *am I doing enough for our children?*

Not just: *should they be taking ballet/ football/ chess/ road safety/ origami classes?*

I jest people, relax, our kids don't do any classes!

Or: *how many chores is it acceptable to ask a mid-sized child to do, and how authoritarian does one need to be to ensure these happen?*

No, I'm talking about in the bigger picture sense, things like: *are they turning into good people? How much should they know about sex and at what age? Are they getting enough life experience? What if they don't have any spiritual practices?*

You know, small fry stuff like that which swirls round most parents' heads most days.

But even more frequently I think: *now what are we going to do?*

As in... we've got three hours till my husband gets home. They're bored. I don't have the energy to do anything creative or practical with them. It's raining. WTF are we going to DO to survive the next three hours without mass slaughter?

But then, as I was preparing to lead our women's group on Sunday, a lightning bolt struck that I just have to share with you.

There are only, truly two things I need to do as a mother:

To find my own center.

And to hold the space.

End of story!

Truly!

(Now this is the embarrassing bit where having bigged it up, you're like: "Durgh! of course, Lucy!") But I've started so I'll finish!

Sure, we all know, on one level that being a 'good' parent is nothing about the amount of play dough or painting or nature walks we do with them. We know it in theory, but many of us don't know it on a gut level, in a way that informs our everyday decisions.

That is why this revelation was nothing short of a bolt of lightning from the blue. It united a number of previous observations I have made in the science lab of extreme parenting – otherwise known as my daily life.

So, I notice that when I am below par, tired or ill, that the children go all jangly – as though they can no longer feel their energy being held by me, and so they are pushing the boundaries on every side to try and find where they are, to feel safe. This is the unseen work of parenting, but that which really counts. We can't really SEE when it's being done, but it is really obvious in its effects when it's not.

The equations go something like this. . .

Mama sick = mad kids. Mama tired = evil kids.

Mama happy = happy families.

This is why self-care is so important. It's not just feel-good twentieth century mumbo jumbo. It directly contributes to the wellbeing of the entire family.

Holding space takes energy. Concentrated energy, for those of us who are not, this year at least, fully enlightened beings.

Sometimes holding our center in the midst of the mundane is a lot trickier than in crisis, when the choice is starker: hold your center or freak out.

There are times when I know that holding my center was all I can do. With my daughter's big fall. In birth. With other of the children's injuries and illnesses. With many tantrums. Finding my center. Allowing myself to remain there as everything goes on. As fear and sadness and anger and despair, and not knowing what to do swirl around me.

By holding the space I mean being really, deeply present, emotionally there. Not adding any emotional stuff to the party. Being as pure and transparent and there in the moment as is humanly possible. Being totally there for them. Being responsive, flexible, breath by breath.

Holding the space often means physically holding too. Just holding, not fixing, not clinging. Just body to body, heart to heart, offering the comfort of your presence.

And when I can keep my center, I can hold the space, breath by breath – hold it so that everyone else feels safe to be the way that life is making them at that moment – then I am doing my sacred job as mother. I am being their womb space, their soft place to fall, their mother-soul, their advocate. I am there, completely, for them.

But when I am off center, I cannot do this. When I am tired, overwhelmed, anxious then I react. I am pulled into the emotional storm. Or I am trying to escape – mentally or physically.

Life has been hard with tantrums and sick kiddies these past weeks. Sometimes I find my center, and hold the space, and fulfil my sacred role in a way that I am proud to call myself their mother.

And often I don't. And I feel shame and regret.

But now I know, in really simple terms, what it is I am aiming at, it makes it seem more doable.

And perhaps it will for you too!

The mother-soul

The moment a child is born, the mother is also born. She never existed before. The woman existed, but the mother, never. A mother is something absolutely new.

Rajneesh

What does it mean to be a mother?

I often struggle for the words to address this question, to adequately describe the profound transformation that occurred to me more than seven years ago.

It is as though when each cell of my children's bodies was formed within my womb, a corresponding cell of my own body was also transformed. In building a baby, I also built a mother. In mothering my children, I also nourish my own mother-soul. Becoming a mother is a two way mirror of co-creation.

Mothering for me has been a profound experience. A soul-shaping, deeply fulfilling, essential process. It is what I am about. I was not expecting this.

Let me be clear, mothering is not my everything. And it certainly doesn't come easy. Rather it challenges me daily to my core, it has chased me to utter despair and back again. With each child I have had, I mourned the prolonged putting aside of certain parts of myself. I cherish little pockets of respite from the endless mental and physical intrusion on my previous, independent sense of self, which the daily reality of mothering requires. I do not find that the daily drudge of mothering comes easy: I do not feel like a natural. But the soul side – that is different.

My mother-self is like my twin soul which I never knew I had until it was activated by the tiny germ of a child growing within my womb. I was birthed as a mother on the day I birthed my first baby. My experience of mothering is what Jung would have called an archetypal experience. Being a mother is part of my being. I am a mother in every cell of my body, at work, across the oceans, in my deepest sleep.

Once we have experienced this transformation on a personal level, we suddenly recognize it in others – our friends, our sisters, our own mothers, as well as every wolf, cow and cat that we see. We understand what drives her, her basic motivation, her deepest feelings for her children.

And know that I do not speak lightly of this. I know what it is like for the mother-soul not to be awakened. I know that whilst it is generally a natural occurrence, it does not always happen. A shock to the mother, the separation of mother and child, a traumatic birth, depression – all can delay or sever this bond.

I have experienced the awakening of the mother-soul twice. But I have three children. For my middle child I did not experience it. For three years I simply acted as if, I consciously went through the motions of mothering, of being the matrix, with my head, rather than from my heart. The soul sense of mothering was not there. It was horrible to feel detached, especially knowing how it felt to be attached to my firstborn. But it emerged. Suddenly, one day I was aware that it was there. It is a little more tentative than my other two, but it is there, the mother-soul.

***

Matrix is the Latin for womb, and the root of our English words matter, material and mother. It is also our term for energy field or underlying fabric of being. This feels instinctively right as a description of what being a mother is, for me: I am a matrix, a sustaining and nurturing energy force. A feeling which the acts of natural birth, breastfeeding and co-sleeping have all acted to reinforce.

Joseph Chiltern Pearce, author of *The Magical Child*, explains that the mother offers three things to the developing child: "a source of possibility; a source of energy to explore that possibility and a safe place within which that exploration can take place." This confirms to me that mothering is really energy work – requiring soul energy and physical energy – which is why it is both as challenging and rewarding as it is.

One of the most insightful discussions of the spiritual energy of mothering that I have discovered is in the writing of Rudolf Steiner. He developed the idea of a Madonna's cloak, which surrounds the child for their first three years, experiencing itself as still part of the mother. It is "the out-streaming of the mother's soul [which] can be pictured as forming a protective cloak around the baby, radiating love and protection. For the young child [the] Madonna's cloak is a spiritual reality. It enfolds him in warmth and deeply affects him." (Joan Salter, *The Incarnating Child*.)

As mothers our fundamental role is that of being physical and spiritual energy in which our child may grow and develop their own vital energies. This takes courage, wisdom, consciousness and a conviction about something which our culture has little understanding of.

Another vital part of our journey as mothers is to learn to wean with love. To build our children's own physical and spiritual strength, so that they are flourishing. And then, to learn to pull our own nurturing energy back, little by little, in an age appropriate way, until they are able, in good times, to sustain themselves, safe in the knowledge that they might return to the matrix at any time. This is the goal of mothering.

In order to do this, our sacred lesson is to learn to nurture and sustain ourselves. We cannot nourish another if we deplete ourselves. If the river runs dry, the crops will fail. Always, always, a mother must return to self-care, to nurturance of herself: she must prioritize tending the wellspring of her own health, her body, her soul. So when we breastfeed we must ensure we are well-nourished, well-hydrated and well-rested. We must nourish our spirits in whatever manner calls us. Health for mother and child rest on the balancing of energies, of giving and receiving.

Mothering is sacred work, spiritual work, hard work. As mothers we get to be co-creators in the magic of the universe. Let us honor this task, ourselves and our children. Let us provide a culture and environment for the mother-soul to flourish: for ourselves, for all mothers, for our children, for the future of our species.

This is my contribution to the La Leche League GB anthology Musings on Mothering (2012).

Speaking for birth

"How can I speak for birth?"

That was my question, back when I first felt called to do birth work. To advocate for birth. Natural birth. Birth as she has always been for millions of years. Generation after generation. Nothing weird or hippy. Nothing worthy. Just the miracle of biology which is birth. Donkeys, goats, dolphins and cats do it: nothing weird there. That's all I wish for women, is to experience the magic of life, the wonder of birth.

We have been told that birth is dangerous, uncertain, not to be trusted. And that birthing like animals is beneath us. We need to be saved from that.

When in fact the opposite is true. Natural birth gave me back to myself. It was a revelation to me. And it has become a large part of my life's work. I truly want to help more women share this most fundamental and natural of experiences, because in our medicalized birthing world this is not an inevitability, but a rarity.

I started to mentor childbirth classes but came up against a sticking point: for me, natural birth is the greatest gift, but I'm not allowed to say that. I'm not allowed to say that because people do not want to hear it. I have to pretend that it's all OK. That one thing is much the same as another, so that mothers do not feel judged if they 'try' and 'fail'. And the chances of this are high in most hospital births, especially with epidurals and inductions and the cascade of interventions which follow. C-sections are running at 20-30%. C-section is NOT a failure. But it spells the end of a natural birth, and a challenge to fight for subsequent ones. And that makes me feel very, very sad for the mother.

You see, we're there. . . I want to speak for birth, but I do not want to upset those who cannot, did not, have her. My heart weeps for all those who wanted her but could not. For the second time mum who feels that her previous dreams of a natural birth were just naivety. That is what inspires me to write and talk about it more. But it also makes me bite my tongue. I must not be seen to be foisting my strange natural birthing beliefs on others, to be judging them when they choose differently.

It is a great challenge. Because most women don't want to hear. Or they don't believe you. Or they think you were just lucky. Or mad to even try. Or they think to birth outside of a hospital setting is nice in theory, but not in practice. And whilst my soul calls out to them clear and loud, my voice stutters and stumbles.

Mother, mother, I want to say. I know you are scared. I know you cannot begin to believe how birth might be and if even if you can birth your baby at all. I know the gnawing, overhanging sense of the unknown and the uncontrollable which keeps you awake at night and haunts your days. I know that death and danger camp close to your door. But I know that life is there too. With birth as her herald. She is majestic. She is the crashing waves, the tiger's roar, the monkey who clings to her baby. She is in your every cell. She is you. You are her. There is nothing that you need to know: simply surrender yourself to her dance as she shakes your baby free.

You can do it. . . but you do not know this. And neither do most of the staff in any hospital. And this is the problem. They go by clock time, by the beep beep of the monitor, the change of shift, the specter of insurance pay-outs, by what they see, not what you feel. They do not understand labor time, they do not trust their hands and heart, your body and your strength. In the fear of death, of the uncontrollable, they can extinguish the possibility of the miracle of birth.

You, dear one, must go within, deep within, to find your core, your tiger roar, your power, your steel. You must hold tight to this as the waves of birth wash through your body. In the light, the noise, the fear of an unsafe public birthplace you might be washed away. You need the freedom to keen and groan and sway with the winds of birth. To hear your birth song, the song in your heart that you never knew was there, which you begin to sing aloud as your baby descends. Through these Gates of Fear and Doubt, Surrender and Exultation, you, dear mother, walk to meet your baby. This is the testing ground of your courage.

Believe in yourself. Surround yourself with others who believe in you. Believe in birth too. You can do it. And when you do it, then you will truly know your own power.

Pain

There is a moment in every birth. Quite close to the beginning where I say.

"Oh £%*! I remember this!"

Pain.

White hot, searing, bone crunching pain.

This is what I feared before I gave birth.

Curses to the hippy women who deny it. Curses to me who denied it to others. These are surges. . . of pain!

And yet, somehow I learned to sail the ship of my body-mind through its seas undrugged and unscathed.

After the last contraction when you think you might die. The last push which shears your being in two with its ferocity. When you think you cannot possibly do any more. And then you don't have to. It is already done. And you see the magic of the child you have brought forth. And you think – I could have done that for ages longer.

This is what the magic of hormones soothes away in the soft pink afterglow of love which follows a birth.

Suddenly all that is real is life and love and perfection and joy.

Until next time.

But here I am once more, a sea of contractive waves rolling in. And it's just me.

"Oh £%*!"

Layer cake

Life for me as a mother is like a layer cake: I just can't jam it all in my mouth in one go. I can't savor its wholeness, the harmony of its completeness, the careful balance of the textures and flavors. I get all of one, and then all of another. I love it, I hate it. I want it forever, I can't bear another second. . .

I taste the tartness of tantrums and tiredness and despair at my lot. Red and raw as raspberry jam, the pips get stuck in my gums.

The rich oozing chocolate love of adoration hits me at another moment. They are edibly good, my little cherubs. I shower them with kisses and thank the heavens for all my blessings.

Andthenthere'slotsofboringsponge–laundry,washingup,nagging them to get dressed, and brush their teeth, and for the hundredth timeliedownandgotosleep and don'thityoursistersaysorry and whatdoyouwantinyoursandwichtoday?

And then there's the Smarties on top that you want to pick off and pop in your mouth, all at the same time – baby curls and toddler kisses and flowers picked from the garden just for you.

And more flipping sponge. Who the hell likes sponge anyway? Tidy the toys, sweep the floor, nag over homework, where's your shoes, Idon'tknowanddon'tcareifthereareanymatchingsocksright now – we're late – again!!!!!

And some bitter coffee gucky stuff – who makes these bloody cakes anyway? I don't like coffee icing, didn't order coffee icing, you can take these kids and give them to someone who cares because right now I am SO done with being a mother – oh sorry, coffee icing, yes, yuck!

Oh, more sponge cake, my favorite!

And light fluffy vanilla icing – whipped like the white clouds that float lazily over the summer beach where we lay on our backs and listen to the timeless chatter of children's voices as they build castles in the sand, and solve the world's travel problems by aiming at Australia, straight through the center of the earth. Those moments when time goes slow, and you have no timetable but your own, and you pinch yourself because these beautiful golden creatures are actually yours.

That.

That is parenthood.

In cake form!

So now you have it, you can eat it!

And don't complain if it makes you fat!

tenderness

Tenderness is one of the most beautiful and commonly identified emotions of motherhood. It is the feeling of love and nurturing and gentle care, hormonally created by our bodies in the form of oxytocin, in order to bond us to our babies.

Bye bye baby

The time has come.

Weaning time.

But it is bittersweet, as weaning always is for me. I love the closeness, yet I resent the being tied and demanded of to this extent. I never want it to end on a bad note, nothing drastic. We will follow our own internal timetables. But I know the sadness will come, and the hormones will slump. There will be tears as well as relief. One of the final chords of babyhood, our intimate physical connection, will be cut. Not visible like the umbilical cord, the first cutting, but just as real.

She doesn't need milk any more, she can eat caterpillars with a fork now!

As this is my last baba the feeling is even harder. This will be my last feed ever. But I am not prepared to go on and on, just for fear of this sadness. The tears are rolling now. It is always a big step. And I know from friends who have weaned at seven months, two and a half years or four and a half, this bittersweetness is always there. The visceral tug of the heart strings. I do not think that extending this will dissipate that sadness. It is inevitable. That is the nature of weaning.

But I am giving myself permission to, and ask that you respect this. I am not looking for people to encourage me to feed longer. I need to bring my energy back for myself, I am so drained and constant feeding and night waking is draining me beyond my capacity. She is 16 months. She has had a good stretch. My other two were 25 months and 16 months when I weaned them. In hindsight 25 months was too long for me. I feel comfortable that I have given them each a great start in life, but I do not need to be so tied to them. I feel a change of energy in feeding as they enter the toddler zone, a level of control that comes from their need to feed. A need I would prefer to meet in cuddles and kisses and other forms of togetherness.

I have made a decision to have an end of baby celebration when we wean, a kind of naming party – as we don't christen our babies. We will bury her placenta (which is still in the freezer) and rename her – she has been 'Baby Ash' since she was born. When I stop feeding her she will become her full name, Aisling (which means dream or vision in Irish), to mark her move out of babyhood and into little-girl-dom, and as a way of marking our movement out of being parents to babies for the past six years.

We will take each day at a time, it may be two weeks or two months hence. But I feel the change coming. She is more and more like a little girl every day – solid, cheeky, playing with the family, new words are tumbling out to surprise us almost daily. She is leaving her baby days behind and this is one more step on that road. I hope this ritual will help us all move forward in celebration and give us a chance to process our sadness. It will symbolize another step on our journey as parents, for us as a family, with three children, rather than two and a baby. And it will be a special day for Aisling, our sweet dream, herself.

Breastfeeding

I am approaching the end.

Six years of breastfeeding. And I couldn't tell you what I feel. I want to be done. And I am sad that it is. It is something which I had never done before. . .

And will never do again.

That is so final. It is big in my heart. Too big to write. And that is strange for me. The only way in is through the little things, the details.

What has breastfeeding been to me?

Lots of wakeful nights.

A quick soother – of me and my babies – the gentle flood of calming oxytocin and prolactin coursing through our veins and smoothing out our tiredness and frustrations.

A warm glow.

A drag and bind.

The feeling of being Madonna and child, and being scorned and discomfiting others.

Swollen breasts the sizes of planets when the milk came in.

Sweet and juicy – and sucked dry and gnawed raw.

Being she who holds complete satisfaction.

Being female – dripping sweet nectar abundance – a miracle of nature.

Aching breasts longing for a child when I am out and a feed is due.

Bitten nipples, blocked ducts, biting my tongue from screaming in the early days, an aggravator of after-pains, the most natural feeling in the world, spots and scratches from grubby little picking fingers, stretch-marks and a cup size almost half way through the alphabet.

Golden warmth.

A soother for sore teeth, feverish limbs, shocks and knocks, tiredness, hunger and tummy bugs.

A holding closeness like no other – love in action, the heart chakra open and embracing.

Blessed relief and gratitude when they milk my engorged breasts.

A food supply – one that has been given on buses, trains, planes, leaning sideways in a car, snuggled in single beds, in the crack between mattresses, in slings, in parks, in shops, in restaurants and dinner parties, on beaches, stretched out on the sofa in front of the TV, curled up in the armchair with the computer, standing, sitting, squatting, in toilets and children's parties. I have fed my children wherever they needed it.

Something I have never regretted, not really, but which I've sworn I'd stop many times – that I have resisted and loved in almost equal measure since the very beginning.

Something which my children adored – it was the most important thing in each of their lives bar none. Until it wasn't.

Something which they will never remember – and that makes me sad.

A soul and body commitment to them – however rough it got.

The natural way to feed my babies.

Something that felt good and right to me.

Something whose time has come.

Finished.

The lost art of lullaby

I have just come downstairs from singing my children to sleep. What a wonderful experience. No fighting or tears, just two sweaty little bodies gradually growing limper in my arms as slumber and song intertwined and lulled them, my words perhaps painting the start of their dreams.

Bedtime here is usually books and cuddles, sometimes a CD. Perhaps ours is the first generation not to soothe our children to sleep with song. We have so many other options. And so can forget the power and the simplicity of our mother voices, singing the songs of our ancestors, passing on melody and words to the next generation.

I am a writer and yet I find storytelling almost impossible. I want my children to experience the joy of story outside of books, but find I have storyteller's block! Tonight, however, I realized that for me, the storytelling urge comes through song. Interestingly, that is how knowledge, wisdom and history have been passed through the generations: through the medium of song.

Each of my children from their first weeks of life had their own personal song with their name in it. My son, Timmy Solas Shanti had the sea shanty, "Bobby Shafto's Gone to Sea" changed for his name. Merrily, of course, gets "Row, Row, Row Your Boat", and Aisling has had "Goodnight Irene" adapted to her name. They each love their songs and regularly request them. I am never allowed to sing just one, always the trio, they insist upon this fairness themselves. And they have to be sung in descending order of age!

I have also developed a repertoire of songs which I have sung to them since they were young when walking the country lanes with them in a sling or buggy trying to get them to go to sleep. Not only must the tune be soothing, but I want the words to be meaningful. I sing to their souls, and pass on my mother wisdom this way, under the radar, all too aware that even little children do not like to be lectured on life by their parents: "Que Sera Sera"; "You Are My Sunshine"; "Peace Like a River"; "Summertime"; "Somewhere Over the Rainbow"; "Moon Shadow"; "Edelweiss" and "So Glad I'm Here" are my classics.

But this night I took it further. I summoned to memory my favourite hymns from childhood: "All Things Bright and Beautiful"; "Amazing Grace"; "Morning Has Broken"; "Swing Low Sweet Chariot" – songs of soul, god and nature, songs to make the spirit and voice soar together.

For years I have wondered how to pass on my own understanding of the spirit to them. We do not go to church together, I have too many issues with organized religion, and yet I always loved the music.

At Cambridge I went to church twice a day on a Sunday to lose myself in the exquisite beauty of my college choir in the ancient chapel. I love to sing and yet, since being told, aged twelve, that I couldn't by a peer, I have always been shy of singing alone. I have a recurring fear of opening my mouth and my voice drying up. The panic of singing alone was so great that I left drama school a nervous wreck after the first year, knowing that my first task in second year was to stand on stage and sing alone. And so I find it freeing to sing my children to sleep. It doesn't have to be perfect.

As a mother I find singing to my children is a primal calming mechanism. The sound of my voice and gentle rhythm calm both baby and mother. Hearing my voice, being aware of my breath, song draws me both deeper into myself and yet lets me float away, it engages my brain, swirling with thoughts and demands that I concentrate. It gives me new words. It takes the harshness, anger, frustrations away and soothes me.

I have always dreamed of being a family that sings together, not quite a Von Trapp family, but one which sings together as a way of being together. I have a friend who sings with her grown up siblings at every family event: weddings, christenings and funerals, they sing as one. For me there is magic in a group of people joined in song, a spine-tingling sensation, which is made more profound when the people are related. I dream for my family this way of shared expression. To this end I make sure we sing together regularly during the day which they love. I dream of a family choir, like one I read about in an alternative parenting magazine, where whole families gather together, perhaps one day a month to sing together, men and women, children of all ages, descants and trebles, sopranos and basses, all breathing, all singing, all together.

This night music is a tradition I want to build on, one which I hope will live in their aural memories forever, songs to calm and soothe and nourish their spirits. Songs which will become part of their very beings.

This was my Dreaming Aloud column from JUNO magazine, Winter 2010.

Sweeter with you

Two weeks after the trauma of almost losing our third child (see "Almost" p.186), we had the most wonderful family holiday in the UK – sunshine, picnics in the park, full days at the playground, ice creams and water play, pond dipping, seeing loved ones, a festival and the highlight for us all – a ride on a real steam train.

And all the time as I watched Aisling swing and laugh and run and play (oh how bright she is, how quickly she is developing) the sentiments of this poem ran through my head. . . so I wrote it down. And wanted to share it with you all – all who sent a text, a message, an email, a card, a present, left a comment, for each of you who have asked since how she is doing, how we are doing: this is how it is. . .

For Aisling, three weeks on from "Almost". . .

Your face has healed.
Not a mark or a sign.
And my hands no longer shake.

And so we had a break
Away,
As a family:
Complete.

And you know my love,
It was sweeter with you.

As we watched you dart around the ferry,
And took you out on deck again and again,
Being careful not to
Hold you too close,
So you could feel the sway beneath your own feet,
The wind in your hair.

It was sweeter with you.

As we played in the park,
And camped in the rain.
Watched puppet shows,
And rode the choo-choo train,

It was sweeter with you,
My love,
So much sweeter with you.

With your bouncy curls,
And your cheeky grin,
You beautiful girl,
With your big brown eyes and your
Funny words.

It is sweeter with you,
My love,
So much sweeter with you.

You are the heart of our family
The almost, not quite.
Again and again,
Like a will-o-the-whisp.
You have chosen to stay.

So different in stature, persona and hair,

To your two elder siblings,
Who love you,
We love you, and Granny does too,
And Granma and Granddad,
Just because you are you.
Your very own person,
Even though you're just two.

It is sweeter with you,
My love,
So much sweeter with you.

The memory keeper

One of our sacred functions as mothers is to be our children's memory keepers. To keep mementos of their precious years which they are too young to remember fully themselves.

I realized this more fully when putting boxes away in the attic this weekend.

A little caterpillar vest with stains from newborn nappies, dyed sludge green in its first wash; pretty embroidered dresses that would fit a fairy.

A red jumper for a two-year-old boy with an appliqued yellow digger which he wore as a fluffy haired toddler.

All so impossibly tiny. Now only appearing in photographs, no longer populating our washing line or laundry mountain.

The little red shoes and coat which I bought for a daughter of mine, before I even had a daughter.

Their paper trail of first artworks which litter every surface of our home. Which now are so ubiquitous, it is easy to disappear whole piles of them into the recycling bin. But looking back, we see the evolution of penmanship, imagination, skill and brain development before our eyes. Scribbles evolve into circles through each subsequent drawing. Eyes appear, and arms and legs, then suns and grass, then first letters and attempts at name-writing, and then mummy and daddy, first just blobby heads and dots for eyes, then later each with the correct number of fingers and toes. Our house first just a square, and later with dormer windows and faces pressed against them. Then as the urge to draw begins to falter, T Rexes, knights with intricate chain mail and racing cars.

Precious bits of material memory. The tangible fabric of days gone by. Of bodies that were smaller, hands less able.

Some of these will be passed on to them, to store in their own attics – testaments to their very own past lives. Some perhaps to grandchildren of the future. And some will be kept and stroked and loved all over by an older woman, with tears and smiles, as she casts back over her memories of children long gone.

Living this life you do not notice the changes until you look back. Until you see what was, only then you can you really appreciate the miracle of what is now.

I put these things up with my old university notes, love letters, photographs of a teenage girl with her school-friends, my childhood books, which had, in turn, been kept by my mother for me.

It is a sacred role: passing the material memories down the generations and one I am honored to continue.

ambiguity

Maternal ambiguity is something that we dare not speak of.

We are expected to love, to be in love with, to like our children all the time. This is what 'good mothers' do.

But the reality is not black and white, but more shaded and nuanced. We love our children and can't stand them in a matter of moments. We would die for them and don't want them to touch us again for five minutes. All at the same time. Reconciling these contrastingly strong emotions takes courage and self-assurance. It is this which makes us realize that there is a lot more to motherhood than happily ever after.

The waves and the shore

I am the shore, the stony shore,
Rocky, hardened by time.
Impenetrable.
You, my children, the waves
The ever-crashing, bashing, smashing waves.

The infinite ocean of your possibilities
Leads as far as the eye can see
Sometimes gray and stormy,
Sometimes calm and blue,
Ever changing, ever changing.

Sometimes throwing up seaweed,
Decorating the mothershore in stickiness.
You wear down my edges, weathering my sharp corners,
Rounding me into something more beautiful
and enduring.

Sometimes the storm winds sing so loud I cannot hear my
own thoughts,
You pound so insistently I cannot feel my own body.
I am storm-tossed, wind-blown, wave-washed, all at sea.

But the tide turns, the waves retreat to play on
other shores,
I am still here, and all I can hear is the echo of your roar
Haunting my ears, filling the spaces between my thoughts.

Broken into smaller pebbles, here I lie.
And wait for you,
The tide will turn and back you come to the mother-soul
Seashell souls held close to my stony breast.

Holding tight. . . letting go

Our human problem – how to let go while holding tight,
how to simultaneously cherish the closeness and intricacy
of the bond while at the same time letting out the ravelling
string, the red yarn that ties our hearts.

Louise Erdrich, "Nests"
from The Blue Jay's Dance: A Birth Year

Parenting is a bitter-sweet adventure. Biology and emotion entangle us into a deep attachment to our children. One which biology and culture then demand that we disentangle. Life is a series of weanings.

Seeing my children sleeping I am hit by the largest sadness: I cannot keep them. They are almost more precious to me than my own life. But they are only mine to run alongside, just as the wind and the sea are mine. I can dip myself in their waters, feel them blow through my hair, but then they will be gone. How I long to bottle them, to be able to take them, just as they are now, out of my pocket – the perfect baby, cheeky toddler, zany school boy – whenever I need to, twenty years hence, when the intensity of today's life is gone and my mother heart is sad.

What happened to the wonderful adventures?
The places I had planned for us to go?
Slipping through my fingers all the time
Well, some of that we did, but most we didn't
And why I just don't know.

"Slipping Through my Fingers", ABBA

And yet I have these moments, far more than I want of them, when everything is more than I can handle. They demand my totality, now, now, now. It is too much. I cannot breathe, let alone think. I am submerged under a tumble of children, crawling over me puppy-like too early every morning. I have their precious selves here, now, endlessly nagging for more food or not wanting to go for a walk or drawing on the table. Get me out of here, someone, please save me.

Many call this maternal ambiguity. But that is too vague a word. I feel a depth of love, a soul longing for my children which is unfathomable. And yet, I need to be me, to be free, to run for the hills, to keep my sanity and my physical space intact.

> *In love's dances, in love's dances,*
> *One retreats and one advances. . .*
> *One gives what the other needed, needs or will need*
> *Now unheeded.*
>
> **Black Monday Love Song, ASJ Tessimond**

Attachment parenting has been the buzz word these past few years. With my gentle birthing, sometime sling wearing, co sleeping, long term breastfeeding, stay at home parenting, I practice this. But like many others who walk this path, I am also a practitioner of mindfulness practices which call for non-attachment. Attachment, teaches the Buddha, is the root of all human suffering. This is true. If your child is gravely sick I am sorry, I move on; if my child is gravely sick I am deeply anxious, sad, overwhelmed. The difference is not the reality of sickness, but my attachment to the person as being 'mine' and therefore a part of my own ego which is terrified of its own impermanence and is therefore ever seeking to prove itself as solid, important and real.

> *You are the bows from which your children as living*
> *arrows are sent forth. The archer sees the mark upon the*
> *path of the infinite, and He bends you with His might*
> *that His arrows may go swift and far.*
>
> **The Prophet, Kahlil Gibran**

Most 'attachment' or 'natural' parents, have an experiential understanding of the interplay of hormones such as oxytocin and prolactin on strong maternal bonding. We actively encourage the change in parental brain functioning through the act of attentive parenting. Will the weanings of our children from us be harder, than those less attached? My feeling is not. Because by being responsive and drinking deeply from the cup of parenthood whilst that precious chalice is in our hands, we have less need to regret things later. We were there, really, fully there, as much as we could be, physically, emotionally with our children and ourselves as we all grew and developed. And whilst we would give anything for just one more squidge of our beautiful baby's chubby cheeks, we would not trade the lessons and love that have brought us here now.

And so I find myself here, regretting things in the moment, determining to be more present, more appreciative of this precious time, not to wish a second of it away. And yet I am not perfect, I have other soul yearnings too. The bitter-sweet path of parenting is a good teacher to the body, of attachment, and to the soul, of non-attachment.

This was my Dreaming Aloud column in JUNO magazine, Summer 2012.

The blur

Here, where my life once was, there is a blur.

Where once I needed a diary to plan my days, now it is simply a daze. The sun comes up, I am already awake. The sun goes down, my eyes are open but I am no longer here. My body is numb from tiredness. The receding light says we have made it through another day. But what did we do? What did they learn? Did I pass? How can I know?

Another day dawns. Will it be just another day to get through, or will today be a day to sear itself to my soul? Might it be one of a small collections of memories my child will shuffle through in later years as a defining moment of childhood?

Perhaps it will be a day where a major injury occurs to shred the veneer of mundanity with its scarring rawness. Perhaps a day where the words I say, for good or bad, are recorded forever to be played verbatim in their minds and later in a psychiatrists chair. Perhaps all it will be is a yellowed leaf swirling through a shaft of sunlight which makes them feel they saw an angel. We cannot know.

We live on faith alone.

Each moment just like another, and yet so totally unique in its potential. And here we are. The pile of laundry, dishes stacked by the sink, puzzle pieces on the floor and a day ahead. What will it hold?

happy days

Summer days. . . free and easy. . . no compass but our own. A life lived to our own heart beats and desires.

Warmth in our bones, sun on our skin, sand in our sandwiches and fresh strawberry muesli for breakfast, with a dash of double cream.

Lazy walks accruing nature's bounty: tiger striped caterpillars, roadside barley, flowers in hot pink and burnt orange.

And lots of scrumped fruit: tiny tart wild strawberries from the crumbling wall on the way up the road. White peaches from my father's greenhouse, dripping juice down our arms as we suck and smile. Ruby red raspberries and loganberries the purple of a bruise.

A fairy girl throwing pots. Lots of pots by us all – a whole new generation of Pearce potters in the making! Hurray!!

A little girl hanging on to her mama's skirt. The mama who said, "stop hanging on to my skirt, it drives me crazy!" The little girl responds, "But I love you mama!"

Building sandcastles, and knocking them down again. Popping down to the beach after supper – just because we can!

And left-over chocolate birthday cake.

Happy days!

depression

Depression within the maternal experience is common, yet shockingly under reported. It may emerge during pregnancy, after the birth, or during your years of mothering.

I have experienced all three, and with the exception of two days, completely unmedicated, so it has been deeply challenging at times. It is so hard to judge – how much is 'normal' hormonal effects of pregnancy and birth, and how much is real depression? How much should I be coping versus how much am I coping? And the clincher – so I'm depressed – but what can be done?

In reality when you are pregnant or breastfeeding your options for medication are limited. And for most women the amount of extra support they can get is also limited, unless things get really bad.

But finding support is crucial – be it from an advice line, a sympathetic doctor or alternative practitioner, your partner, a friend or family. Or preferably all of them. Reaching out is often the hardest, but the most effective, way to break the spell.

The depression of motherhood can break our shells open to love deeper than we could ever have dreamed.

The baby blues

The first time I found myself pregnant it was a bolt from the blue. It was by no means an unwanted pregnancy, but nor was the timing 'perfect'. Instead it uprooted all our career plans and put into question our graduate studies. So when I began feeling low and shaky and bursting into tears at the drop of a hat, sobbing my way through a great New Year's party, I didn't worry too much. I was in shock, of course I was feeling kind of wobbly. The post natal depression which I was dreading, which my mother had suffered from, never materialized.

Two years later, my second pregnancy was planned and I was beyond ecstatic to see the blue line emerging on the test. So when those same feelings hit me at six-and-a-half weeks I was floored. I felt like my body was possessed by a malevolent alien being: it was all I could do to get out of bed for a couple of hours at a time, and most of the time I just got as far as the TV – my normally busy days flew out the window. My mind was dark and brooding. I was weepy and angry. I had no energy, and saw no one except my husband and son. On top of this I felt queasy every waking moment, I dreaded eating. At my lowest I spent a weekend vomiting. It was like PMS plus depression plus jet lag and food poisoning.

It is hard to admit I felt like getting rid of myself and my much wanted baby: the feeling of irrational terror, a need to end it all, so familiar from my last pregnancy. And yet when I looked outside my dark bubble, my life was as perfect as it will ever be. My rational mind knew that I was OK, it was just a massive surge in hormones, and that I wanted this baby. My dark side was telling me if I could just get rid of it, all this would stop. And yet by eight and a half weeks it seemed to begin to lift. Where a day before it had seemed hopeless, suddenly there was a light at the end of the tunnel. But in reality I did not feel myself for the whole of the pregnancy. Nor for a few months afterwards. There was just an enduring numbness, a lack of connection.

But depression proper hit in after baby number three. Despair. Is this what my life has become? Every day I pulled myself through the day by my finger nails. Taking a walk along the cliffs with my three children, all they could think about was stuffing their mouths with blackberries, whilst I entertained secret fantasies of throwing myself off the cliffs.

The hardest thing about maternal depression is the sense that you shouldn't feel this way. It is like you are watching your own life, unable to participate in it, numbed to its joys, their taste dissolves on your tongue without trace. The kisses that are showered on your body fall on numbness. The worse you feel the worse you feel about feeling that way. You see a friend who is desperately wanting to get pregnant, another who has miscarried, and you feel bad for feeling bad. But still it doesn't stop.

You feel like a suitcase which has burst, shedding its contents in public. You try to hold it all together, but at every moment of every day it threatens to burst again.

You try everything – thinking positive, sleep, anti-depressants, herbal supplements, walks outside, seeing friends. Nothing helps.

And then, one day, the shaking subsides, a laugh bubbles up, a feeling strikes a chord. And then blankness returns. But that moment has given you hope.

And one day, in the not so distant future, you look back and see, that zombie woman reflected in the window was me. But she is gone. And I am here once more.

A version of this article appeared in Modern Mum magazine.

Failure

I cannot shift this feeling of failure.

It is as though I can see my perfect mother-self through a dark mirror. She who is always patient and kind. Who always has a nourishing snack to hand, and lots of energy to do messy craft projects.

She was there too at my births – she could do it quieter, with less complaint. She could have done it quicker. She would have felt pure love at the birth of her first daughter rather than strange detachment.

She flows with milk, and would not have had a moments bother with her supplies.

And as for sleep, she would have gently rocked her sleeping child in her arms, crooning sweet lullabies in his ear, rather than pacing the floor, wishing, longing for him to be asleep so she could watch the episode of her favorite cookery program which started twenty minutes ago.

She shifted her baby weight instantaneously, if she put it on at all.

Her babies sleep all night, and wake with a smile to kiss her glowing cheek, before walking hand in hand down to a gleaming sun filled kitchen.

She is the good one, and I am the ugly sister. Oh, how I long to be her. I see aspects of her in other mothers, and snarl. Sometimes I see her fully fledged and run home to hide my tears of anguish.

Not Normal
otherwise known as mothering with mental illness

I am Not Normal. That's the truth I've been running from for years.

And it hurts.

If I'd known then, what I know now, I wouldn't have had three children.

There, there's the rub. Wouldn't have had those three sweet creatures. Wouldn't have imposed myself on them as their mother. If I had known that in fact I was Not Normal.

(Whoa there, don't even start with your anodyne "but who is normal?" response. . . I am venting, so hear me out! It's kinda fun! No need to make me feel better or sprinkle fairy dust on me here.)

If I'd have known that what I thought were my grumpiness and moodiness and irrational ability to freak out at everything were actually the co-morbid triplets of depression, anxiety and migraines, and they were lifelong, I would not have chosen to be a mother.

Because motherhood for the normal is hard. It is long. Relentless. It requires energy and patience and the ability to at least try to love unconditionally.

But when you're Not Normal. . . it's several degrees harder. Promise!

It requires hormonal upheaval which triggers episodes. It causes massive sleep deprivation which trigger episodes. It requires consistency. It requires that you put the care of another at or above the care you give yourself. And when there are three others, and you have a lot of your own needs. . .

It sucks. And you muck up a lot.

You know what, I feel angry. And let down. That no doctor, despite me mentioning every time I was asked about family histories, ever picked up on it. Never. That the midwife, when I tried admitting, which took great courage, how shaken I was feeling during pregnancy and after birth, despite knowing my history, told me to pull my golden cloak round me.

MY FLIPPING GOLDEN CLOAK WOMAN?! There's something seriously wrong with me, this is Not Normal and you're talking about golden cloaks. It took me over a year to get up the courage to tell another medical professional that I really wasn't coping. A year of serious, serious struggling. And the medicine he gave me took me to a whole other wacky level of Not Normal – so once again I was alone with it. Story. Of. My. Life.

I don't feel like sharing events. But there were events during pregnancy and post-partum that should have been red flags to the medical establishment. Episodes which were Not Normal. They would have been flags to anyone who knows about these things. But I didn't, and my husband and family didn't. And so we muddled on. Me, and him in our own secret world. Well my secret world of normal make believe – I'm a trained actress, you know. Occasionally I had to let him into quite how Not Normal things were. I'm sure at times he thought I was nuts. . . and I was! It's just no one else realized.

I always thought I just needed to cop myself on. To pull myself together. *Be normal* is my mantra. I study normal people. Do what they do around the edges of my life as a subterfuge. All the time beating myself up internally for not being able to do this Normal thing well enough to make it real for myself, the way everyone else can. I beat myself up for being over-emotional, over-dramatic, feeling too much, being hormonal. In short being overwhelmed, and not coping a lot of the time.

Normal = being able to cope with reality.

Most of the time it feels like I don't. . .

Though someone very clever, and Not very Normal, once said, let me mangle it nicely for you, that "It's a sign of mental illness, not mental health to be well-adjusted to a sick world." I agree. But the Men in White Coats and School Teachers and Tax Inspectors do not. They are the Arbiters of Normal – they are not my folk! I hang with the artists, hippies, dreamers, poets, dancers, mad ones and earth mothers. We dig Not Normal in all sorts of funky ways.

Not coping with Normal does my nut. I really want to cope. I want to be stable and Normal and reliable to the rest of the world, but really for my kids. I really hate that I'm not. REALLY. It cuts me up so bad.

And please don't give me the "but you're such a good mum, your kids are lucky to have you" spiel. Yes, I do better than someone who's struggling with addiction, someone who's abusing their kids. But that's quite a low bar really for a perfectionist.

I am irritable, regularly too tired to do anything, get anxious doing the weekly shop, struggle having their friends over for playdates, struggle socializing with all but my immediate close circle, our house is in chaos, I tend to freak out at birthdays and Christmas, I'm always sick, I can shout and scream, am often distracted. Sure I can be fun, do creative stuff together, a *lot* of creative stuff, I am affectionate and a humorous reader of stories and singer of songs. But really, I feel quite often that they have quite a bum deal. It's hard enough being like this, feeling like this, but then feeling guilty about the impact that this has on others. That triples sucks. Especially when you super-love those people. I have experienced this from both sides now. I know how it sucks both ways. Yup, woo-hoo I'd like to receive my Buddha certification, I've passed my test in General Compassion and can bugger off to hippie heaven.

But instead I'm still here, making amends for recent crappy behavior, pulling myself through cups of tea that I've been avoiding, trying to focus on school uniforms, and brushing teeth, and stacking dishwashers.

When really I would much prefer to be in my own little bubble with a book, Pinterest, a pen and some paper. All the time.

I struggle with how much they need from me still, and can just see how many more years into the future it stretches. As I said. . . if I knew then, what I do now I would have made very different decisions. But that's the thing about having kids. You can't really make decisions afterwards, except ones that cut like a knife, and so you're stuck struggling. Knowing you want better for them. Knowing you can't deliver. Knowing that most of the time your crapness is better than nothing. Yes, what a heartening thought – my crap presence is, 95% of the time better than my total absence. Cheering!

But I love them and I wish them a Perfectly Normal mother who adores ironing, has a shiny kitchen sink and dispenses neatly matched socks along with pithy words of advice. Someone who delights in cooking dinner for visiting children and driving hordes of kids to noisy events. The parent who always wants to listen to their piano recitals, and can break up fights without having a tantrum herself. The mother who can pick out just the right gift for their friend's birthdays and gives two hoots if their outfits match. I wish them the mother I wanted to be, I thought I was going to be when I started sprogging.

I feel angry, and sad. Sad for me, for my husband, and most of all for my kids, who really don't deserve to have to differentiate what is really me and what is my illness. I have tried to explain it in simple terms, what this illness is, and what my true feelings for them are. I try regularly. It tends to garner blank looks or be brushed off. My Not Normal is Normal for them! That makes me sad. . . and happy too. But with the added awareness that

Not Normal passes down families and a sneaking suspicion of the reality that it has, I try to model openness and honesty in the face of this hugeness within which I live. It comes out as a strange mix of apologies, snot and fake blasé matter-of-factness.

But now at least I know, when I see others enjoying motherhood, blooming during pregnancy, doing OK to keep house, that yes, actually there *is* something wrong with me. I'm officially Not Normal. Any of the Arbiters of Normal could prove that to you. I just keep my head down and out of sight so they can't. Arbiters of Normal can be malicious sods to the Not Normalers of this world.

It's a kind of dance we do. We know we're Not Normal, and so do they. But as long as our Not Normalness is still within the realms of Normalness they'll leave us alone. So we learn to do a good show of Normal 101 to avoid detention, drugs, scalpels, shocks and separations.

And meanwhile daily life continues as it always does. Have kids, try to be Normal. Hate being Normal. Can't do Normal. Feel like you're a crap mum. Repeat ad infinitum. Have good day. Believe it is your new Normal. *You* can do it. . . Oh, no. actually you can't.

Meh!

See you in the introverted artist area in the red tent at the hippie festival of dreams, far from the unsuspecting eyes of the Arbiters! I'm the one with the flouncy skirt curled up with a book. Looking most definitely Not Normal – a fact which I've always secretly enjoyed about myself!

Up. . . and down

"Everything is sex!" I said as we drove down the mountainside, Prince blaring on the stereo.

The forests had a glow about them. The patterns in the foliage jumping out in 3D like one enormous zentangle. I understood everything suddenly, it seemed. Everything was so clear, so fluid and golden. My body too. Liquid honey. Tastes, sights, feelings brighter and clearer. I squeezed his hand delighted to be here, to be alive. The Universe loved me. I was in love with every atom of life. Heaven was on Earth.

And then two days later as though a pin had burst my bubble. Numb darkness and despair. Except there was no pin. A this and a that, but nothing to justify this complete deflation. All was darkness. Hell was here and only I was in it. I felt detached, alone, despised. Everyone hated me. I hated me even more. Thoughts ran and ran through my head. Bad thoughts. I looked out the window at the breath-taking mountain view, snow-capped in the dazzling July sunshine.

Nothing.

I felt nothing. It was as though a gauze curtain had been drawn between me and the world. Its beauty could not touch me. It was just me and the darkness in my head. Nothing else could find its way in.

I slapped myself around the face.

Not something I have ever done before. But better than other options. Something, anything, just to be able to feel again. Come on, snap out of it, I willed myself. Come on. You're on holiday. In a beautiful house. You are surrounded by your family.

Nothing.

I cried and cried. Body shaking. Numb darkness.

Over a few days it became less intense, but lingers on weeks later. Sudden sobs envelop me. A lack of words. Physical tremors. A need to hide. To cower. To run. Paranoia.

This time it was clear to me. All too clear. The high. The low. And no reasons.

I had seen it in others, knew all the signs... But just not in myself. Because my highs are never totally off the spectrum. Instead they are like falling in love. Or being inspired with a new project. Racing thoughts... Being full of enthusiasms. Non-stop talking. Getting the house cleaned in a day. A full week of inspired writing or painting.

I'd previously written the good bits off as creativity, as a rise in libido, as spiritual epiphanies, as finally feeling good after my general grumpiness and impatience... But now I see, oh, so clearly, what this is that I'm dealing with. Many previous events in my life have taken on a totally different color now. I see them more clearly as the symptoms of an illness, not just feelings, events... But connected. The up and down of the see saw. Two parts of the same program. If I own one, I must own the other. Or I must surrender them both for a different existence. Which at this point is my last choice.

I feel pretty foolish for not having seen it before. The great thing about us human creatures is our lack of clear seeing of ourselves. So now I see. And if truth be told I'm scared. Scared of the life sentence. Of the endlessness. Of the way it gets exacerbated by stress. Of not knowing how big the swings could get. Of the legacy I pass on through genes and environment. And of what this means for my kids and husband.

I know from personal experience what it's like to live around. And I feel scared and angry and helpless and ashamed. And maybe it's been obvious to everyone else but me for years. Maybe I was the only one who didn't know.

But now I do. I want to hold it so close. I don't talk about this with anyone. The 'D word' is something I have previously tended to talk about past tense, when it's over. But with this there is truly no over. Ever.

Instead there's a label which feels like a life sentence. . . So I'm choosing not to label it. It's not severe enough to need to. It is rather a temperament. A tendency. A cycle. That can take me and everyone I love with it. So my role now is to manage it. To care deeply, compassionately for myself, and mitigate its effects on those I love.

My first instinct was to keep it from everyone, to hide it, bury it. It's always been my approach when it comes to my adventures with depression. I don't want pity or attention. . . To talk about it makes me feel very vulnerable – personally, professionally, as a mother. . .

But on reflection I think that openness is the best bet. In the long run.

So that's I'm doing here. With my guts in my hands. In your hands. Asking that you not judge me. Or label me. Or write me off either. But in the hope that my openness will help me in my life. And might help others to greater openness in their lives too.

There is no shame in illness. Mental or physical. And with openness comes the potential for acceptance. For empathy. And for healing.

Why getting back to normal is the biggest mistake you can make

When we are sick, depressed, traumatized, grieving, in shock, we long to 'get back to normal'. . . to get back to the way things were before. We yearn for it. And most people around us seem to be urging us to as well.

We long for solid ground. For doing not feeling. For being

functional and contributing. For not impinging on the goodwill of others. To feel calm and whole and good. To feel safe.

Most of all we long to feel safe again. To believe that the world and its people are familiar and friendly. That our body is a safe place to be. That we are, as we used to believe, in control of our own destinies. . .

Rather than being a passenger on a cruel and stomach churning rollercoaster ride with no safety harness that we didn't ask to get on. . . and we can't get off.

We try to get back to normal. For our own sakes. And the sakes of those we love. And we can't. It feels false, like going through the motions. Because it is.

Old normal no longer exists. (And old normal is what got us here in the first place. . .)

We are numb. Our bodies and emotions frozen and in shock. Happiness is a far distant land. Appetite, desire, motivation, joy foreign languages. We marvel in disbelief as to how we ever loved what we did, when we have not an iota of desire for it now. Food, books, favorite movies, friends. . .

Everything is nothing.

Because everything that was 'us' before, has been thrown up in the air, broken into a million pieces. I get a sense that whilst this is a metaphorical way of explaining the dissolution of trauma, it is also in fact a literal explanation, our physical and soul bodies are in states of disintegration and healing. We cannot force normal. . . not for long anyway without further disintegration down the line.

The problem with disintegration is it isn't a clock watcher. In fact it doesn't respect working days, sick leave limitations, religious holidays. . . it just keeps on going. . . until you surrender yourself fully. Until you let go of getting back to normal.

Because the truth that you sense is in fact the reality that everyone including you are in denial of: old normal doesn't exist anymore. That's the reality you're running from.

Getting back to doing things as you've always done them doesn't take away the newly integrated facts – the illness, the loss, the cause of the trauma.

The only way we can heal is by first finding safety. Soothing safety to allow our bodies and minds to be sustained free from panic and fear. Safety so that we can unfreeze. Nurturing, nourishing safety. Only then can we begin to unfurl. Only then can finding a new normal – *creating* a new normal – really begin. A normality that integrates our new reality – internal and external.

But in order to get there we cannot force. Rather we must do the opposite – surrender. Fully. Give ourselves permission to surrender to our new reality, our new selves, exactly as we are now. . . not how we wish it would be.

Loving acceptance is what we need to practice, moment by moment. And we need others' permission too – our bosses, partner's, families', friends' permission to fully surrender to the process. To step out of our heads and into the dynamic, disorienting flow of our bodies, and surrender – surrender to not having the answers, to being afraid, to not knowing the future.

And when we finally reach it, this new normal, we see that everything is changed. Internal. External. . . and yet, when we accept this, we can then see how much everything is also the same.

The threads of the old run through this new reality in small ways and big. . . the comfort blanket of your old reality is here after all, just freshly washed in the laundry of life by Big Mama without your permission! The yogurt stains and daily grime washed out, a ragged bit trimmed off there, the hole stitched up, a different smell. . . same, same but different as they say in Thailand.

Joy

It is easy to getting all moaning and martyrish about motherhood. There is a lot of drudgery. But there is also lots of joy. Little moments and whole days of glory brighter than you can ever remember before, which sear themselves into your heart.

I make sure to celebrate these, and often have a Friday feature called Joy Pockets that celebrates the pockets of joy in my life, which I might otherwise take for granted or overlook in the busyness of life.

Joy pockets

Bedtime family dancing to The Gipsy Kings

Twinkling fairy lights

Baby Ash playing air guitar! Yes, really!

Our boy's pidgin Spanish picked up from said Gipsy Kings CD

Making hot chocolate on top of our wood-burning stove

Playing Christmas carols (badly) on the
piano and everyone singing along

Three little kiddies – practically perfect in every way!
(Thank you Mary Poppins!)

A husband who understands everything – well, me and
WordPress – the two most complex things on the planet

The taste of cherry blossom

The first time I tasted cherry blossom I felt the strands of all the loves in my life made whole in one mouthful.

It was April, and though the blossoms had all been blown by the wind, the taste remained in the exquisite cherry blossom filling of the traditional Kyoto delicacies we were eating in the little Welsh farm house. We sat in silent reverie: myself, my new fiancé, my Japanese friend, her husband. The cherry blossom took each of us back. She to her childhood, he to their wedding, my husband to our recent time in Japan, with memories of temple gardens and meandering bike rides amongst the back streets where geisha walked.

And me, the taste of cherry blossom took me back to the haunting song my father had sung me as a child.

sakura sakura
yayoi no sorawa

Cherry blossoms, cherry blossoms,
Across the spring sky,
As far as you can see.

He had learnt it on his own travels to the Far East. As a young man in the 1960s, he decided to see the world, and headed off to study pottery in Japan for a year. There he learnt the meditative art of Japanese ceramics, the aesthetics, the philosophy of wabi sabi. He returned home, having hitchhiked through the apricot groves of Pakistan, and the coffee houses of Amsterdam, to a rural Ireland which hadn't discovered spaghetti yet, let alone ramen or sushi.

The romance of Japan ran through his veins though. And after his February marriage to my mother some years later, they set off on an extended honeymoon, via America, to see the cherry blossom in Kyoto. And there, in a little traditional ryokan guesthouse, after an evening of hot sake and Kobe beef sukiyaki, I was created on a futon in a room with rice paper walls, and the cherry blossom outside the perfume of my genesis.

As a young child I was immersed in his passion for all things Japanese, but especially the food. On rare trips to London we gravitated towards sushi restaurants, where I would eat cucumber rolls, minus the wasabi and the seaweed. So really it was just cucumber and rice, but I felt so cosmopolitan, sitting on the high stools at the sushi bar, watching the Japanese chef with his flashing silver knives, working with such artistry to carve delicate slivers of seafood for my father's delectation. I would sip miso soup from enamelled bowls, whilst the beautiful waitresses magicked lillies and birds out of paper napkins. I was entranced by the exquisite magic of Japan.

After a teenagehood filled with origami and a soul longing for miso soup, as soon as I had the wings to fly free, I found myself drawn back to Japan, to the country of my soul, to live and work with my boyfriend.

It was a romantic six months of kisses under the fall leaves in Kyoto's hidden temple gardens, sampling the bewildering range of *mochi* rice cakes in tea houses and markets, deciphering menus and a midnight proposal as 100 monks struck the giant brass bell to ring in the New Year. And of course *o-hanami*: the cherry blossom picnic which marked the end of our stay. This venerable Kyoto tradition finds families, students and friends gathering under the cherry trees in the parks and along the Kamo river, eating *mochi*, and drinking plum wine, whilst the candy-colored petals snow gently down onto their heads.

The scent of cherry blossom came home with me, firmly lodged in my heart. At our wedding that summer, we were serenaded by my father and a Japanese friend, with the cherry blossom song. An old school friend gave us a cherry tree, which we kept alive in a pot until we had our own home.

Naturally the first trees we put into our garden were cherry trees.

Now we now have three children of our own, and so it is my turn to bombard them with wistful memories of green tea and rice cakes. My son is seven, and his happiest memory of rare trips to London are of conveyor belt sushi restaurants.

Our children look forward to *o-hanami*, almost as much as Christmas, unaware that it they are the only children in Ireland celebrating it! We watch as the blossom buds swell and split, our own personal harbingers of spring. We spend the first dry spring day preparing sushi for the adults, and *fushi* for the children (rice crispie buns wrapped around jelly snakes). And brew a pot of cherry blossom tea.

And with the blossoms bobbing overhead in the cool spring air, the taste of them on our tongues, my father there beside me, we sing the cherry blossom song. The song of my childhood. The song that my father sang at my wedding. The song that I sang as a free spirit as I cycled around Kyoto before children and mortgages. The song that tastes of cherry blossom in my mind.

sakura sakura
yayoi no sorawa

Cherry blossoms, cherry blossoms,
Across the spring sky,
As far as you can see.

A longer version of this piece appeared in Roots: an anthology of food writing.

An Eden to call our own

Driving into Ballymaloe House gardens, the place where my father and my son both spent parts of their childhood, always feels like coming home. We "drive in the yellow" as my three-year-old calls it. Acre upon acre of gold as far as the eye can see, man-high shocking yellow oil seed rape flowers waving in the wind, line both sides of the drive.

The ripe grape-like bunches of watercolor mauve wisteria greet us, jingling on the austere gray wall of the venerable house. We abandoned the car and meandered down to the lazy river. This is one of the first walks that our one-year-old has done on foot. And so we explored along with her, naming the things we see for her delight, just like Adam, and this our own Eden. . .

The beech woods with their gravity-defying fresh green leaves, each carefully crimped by fairy hands, waved above our heads as we greeted the chickens: red, white, gold, black, fluffy footed and red cropped roosters. Proud white geese stretching their necks in warning. And the regal peacock, resplendent in his iridescence.

Does a peacock know how beautiful he is? He may rattle his tail in temptation at a female, but does he know? If you and I and all our friends were to sit down one day and try to design the most beautiful bird in the world, we wouldn't even get close. From the dainty tiara, to the black and white striped wings, the iridescent blue which belongs on a beetle, not a bird, and the eyes on his tail. He has never seen himself. He probably thinks he looks like a pea-hen, mottled and brown. . . it reminds me of us, we see our drabness, not our beauty or magnificence.

We walked the woods. Bluebells, pink-bells, white-bells in the dappled sun, jingling a tune for fairy ears. Hot pink azaleas and rhododendrons trumpeting their song. Wild garlic, pungent to nose and tongue, calls to be picked.

We tracked a tiger and touched his teeth, hand-in-hand to be sure we were brave enough. We wondered at a waterfall churning bubbles out of thin air. Found a tree that grew handkerchiefs of the finest white silk for kings. And intoxicated ourselves in the scent of damask rose bushes.

For an hour we were as queens. The fairies were our friends. In the garden we met God. And she paints in bright colors.

Candlelight, fairylight, firelight

I know the place where the fairies sleep. Where bonfire sparks make the stars and witches walk.

I know the place where music lives and angels wait.

I know, because I saw them with my own eyes as a child. Colors shimmered, sounds too, and for hour upon hour the laws of nature were richer and deeper, mythical in their proportions. A world of fire and music and story, where the rules of magic reigned. These were not things that I tried to believe, but things I had seen, felt and known in my bones, that made me shiver up my spine, lit up from the inside by magic.

Christmas seemed to inhabit its own realm of magic – where everything was brighter, warmer, fuller, more delicious and abundant than your dreams. Where life glimmered and shimmered by candlelight, fairylight, firelight. When everyone I loved would be gathered in a room together, talking and laughing. Where grown-ups had time to play games in the middle of the afternoon by the fire. A time when music was all around, and piles of presents in shiny paper whispered promise. When every street sparkled with a thousand colored lights, and driving home in the darkness, living rooms glowed with warmth and love and festooned trees

And most magical of all, the portal of wonder, Christmas Eve, when I hung up a stocking, went to bed full of happy butterflies and came downstairs in the cold and dark, to be greeted by a bulging, odd-shaped container of delight, where I would dip my hand in to its Tardis-like proportions, fishing out pencils and books, magic tricks and bubble bath, golden chocolate coins and glowing clementines.

These weren't times when I tried to believe. They were real visits to other worlds within the embrace of this one.

At this time of year especially I long to make magic real for my children. Or rather, to hold the space for magic to emerge for them. In truth I don't know what lights the magic in their souls, what, in their modern and maybe jaded eyes holds the spark of a miracle any more. I don't know which memories have already fused themselves to their cortexes, to live there till they are grandparents. I do not know, but I make it my job, as much as I can, to expose them to magic and miracles – freshly falling snow by moonlight, carols by candlelight, wishing eggs in the woods which the fairies take away, gingerbread houses, bonfires and sparklers in the dark, tooth fairies and Santa Claus.

I kept this magic into adulthood. It truly only fell away this last couple of years, with tiredness, illness, too much work, too much pressure to do it right, not enough money or time, striving, striving to get it right, keep everyone happy, remembering all the details. My soul was stricken, Christmas had lost its glow.

So this year, I am re-lighting the magic of midwinter – it is not about quantity, but about the feeling of abundance. Music singing us into feeling and tasting love on our tongues. And light – candlelight, fairylight, firelight, the sparkle of magic and hope in the midwinter dark and cold. The feeling of togetherness, of joy. Weaving magical memories, suspending the laws of mundanity and bringing magic to life.

Candlelight, fairylight, firelight. . . and magic!

This post was written for the December 2012 Carnival of Natural Parenting about Childhood Memories

So glad I'm here!

"I'm so glad I'm here! So glad I'm here!
So glad I'm here every day!
And love brought me here, love brought me here, here today."

My four-year-old son goes around singing this song, a beautiful rendition of the Elizabeth Mitchell version of the classic gospel track. It makes my soul glow and spine tingle every time I hear it.

Usually it is in the mornings, as we all scramble into the car, late for playschool again, tempers frayed, hair unbrushed, socks unmatching, after the endless hunt for shoes under sofas and the struggle to get three bodies dressed.

I start the car engine, and this song begins to flow through my veins. I take a deep breath and allow the stress to flow out of me.

I drive past the hedges, and see them in their glory, just beginning to wake from their winter slumber, the ruffled birds, the wispy clouds hung in the cool blue sky as if by magic. I glance at my two little munchkins in the backseat, with their haloes of blonde hair, dark chocolate eyes and the most kissable cheeks in the world.

The frustrations and drudgery of motherhood evaporate.

I am so glad I'm here.

Guilt

Guilt is one of the omnipresent factors of motherhood that few of us expect. We feel guilty because we are not there enough, we feel guilty that we need time to ourselves, that we snapped at our children, that we cannot give them everything their heart desires, that our relationship with their father is not as we had hoped. . . each of us has our own heavy weight to our soul.

As the editor of an alternative parenting magazine I deal with this feeling perhaps more than most. It often feels that the 'crunchier' you are, the further you have to prove your credentials. As a magazine you are showing an 'ideal' or 'aspirational' lifestyle, this can be very hard for readers, and editors alike.

Getting over guilt

"Sometimes, I have felt when reading your magazine that it created a sense of guilt, if we were not home schooling or have had our children vaccinated. I am open to debate and enlightenment but not to any guilt promotion. Being a parent is difficult enough."

So wrote a *JUNO* reader to the editorial team.

I whole-heartedly agree.

Being a modern day parent is a job wracked with guilt, especially as the gulf between the alternative and mainstream gapes between every decision you take.

Guilt usually emerges when there is a perceived gulf between our aspiration and our actuality.

I often feel deeply challenged from both sides of that divide – mainstream friends and acquaintances are disgusted (not too strong a word) that I breastfed my first child to over two years of age and share a bed with my babies. I am irresponsible/brave/mad enough to have birthed all three at home, and cranky enough to have deep issues with our educational system.

On the other hand, my more alternative leaning friends are appalled that we tried and failed with washable nappies. Or that I shop at Primark and Tesco, not for everything, or all the time, but I do. We use antibiotics for tonsillitis. We have chosen to vaccinate our children. We watch TV, eat sugar and meat galore, and only some of what we buy is organic.

Every time I write for *JUNO* I am aware of which bits of me are acceptable and which bits to censor. As I do the other way around when I write for the 'mainstream' press. I have learnt, from bitter experience, that I, in all my complexities, am not acceptable.

Most days I find myself walking the guilt tightrope from one end of the day to the other. Everything I say, do, buy, eat is second guessed – "Is this OK?" I ask myself endlessly. For me, for my kids, for the planet, the producers, our bank account, the people around me? If I breastfeed here will people object? If I buy non-organic strawberries. . . and don't wash them? And they're not Irish? If I choose this T shirt? If I respond in this way to my child? If I use that to clean our floor?. . . I think most of you will share this dilemma in some way, multiple times a day.

Once we have reached a level of self-awareness, of consciousness of the possibilities out there rather than simply imitating the status quo, decisions can feel daunting and endless. We want to endear ourselves to others, to live at ease with our friends, family and acquaintances, but how to do this when our choices so directly contradict theirs? How to be when the decisions we make are 'moral' choices and we see them, or they see us, falling far short, and being downright irresponsible?

I feel the need to defend my informed decision to vaccinate. Not tooth and claw, as I once did, to assert myself as right, and the other as wrong, but so that people are aware that it is just that, a well-researched decision. Just as much as the next mother who chooses to defend hers not to vaccinate.

It is deeply challenging, because there are no definitive answers about almost anything. Research and expert opinion once recommended bottle feeding and separation of mother and baby where now they advocate breast and bonding. There are no certainties, no rule books. Just judgment: ours, and that of those around us. Feeling judged when we are struggling to do our best is the path of parenting it seems. We mothers, who are generally at the coalface of bearing and daily caring for our children, are perhaps most vulnerable to it. Society knows this. How to have the most effect on a parent? Make them feel guilty. . .

Guilt is a powerful, insidious tool which has been utilized to great effect by religions throughout history. It is perhaps the greatest way to stunt a human being. And we have learnt to do it to ourselves, to self-regulate our actions daily. It has the power to make us strive harder, higher, better. But it also has the power to shut us down and make us feel so bad that we stop trying altogether.

What medicine can we take from this? The Buddhist teaching of equanimity is always a thought provoking lesson: things are not good, nor bad, they simply are. Once we can allow for this, our ego can detach a little from our own rightness (or wrongness), and we can begin to enter into dialogue or compassionate acceptance, with those who choose differently from us.

The power of guilt, and of judgment, can imprison us firmly in the gaols of our own values. Openness to possibilities is the key to setting us free.

This appeared in JUNO magazine Winter 2012.

The perfect mother

When I was twenty I thought that people should wait until they were perfect to have children. I had seen and felt the damage done by those who were less than perfect. And I wanted to do better.

My sense is that many of us start from this place in our parenting journeys – seeing the shortcomings of our own caregivers and others, our own upbringings in sharp relief to how we would do things. We require nothing less from ourselves than perfection. In the cool light of day we conjure up children in our minds. And we see ourselves, calm, patient and loving. This is how it will be, we tell ourselves. I will do it right.

And so I set it as my (rather naïve) challenge to become the perfect person. I am not quite sure what my deadline was, but I presume it was sometime before my eggs would no longer be viable. I would analyze and control my thoughts, read endless improving books, work hard, control my emotions, meditate, eat right. . .

And then, aged 24, and admittedly a little before perfection had been achieved, my son was conceived.

I did everything I could to be that perfect parent. I planned and achieved a gentle birth, breastfeeding, staying home, gentle sleep solutions, holding my child when he cried, sling wearing, delayed solids. . .

For the first couple of years with just one child it felt like I was achieving just that: I was, if not perfect, certainly the 'good' mother I had always longed to be. After the sleep deprivation wore off we had the sort of golden bond I had always dreamed of.

But one day, somewhere in the midst of mothering a second child, the cracks began to show. Suddenly, I was most definitely *not* the perfect parent. There was not enough of me to go around. Baby puke was no longer charming. Now I was impatient, low on energy, bored with playing tractors and realized, perhaps a little too late, that my calling in life was not soothing small babies.

I was devastated.

If I wasn't perfect, if I wasn't the good mother, then what was I? I must be a bad mother.

And it's hard enough to be a bad mother in your head. But when you think that other people think you're a bad mother. . . Or even worse that you have a 'bad' baby. "Is she good?" strangers would ask of my baby. "Be a good girl!" they would threaten to my little girl and her dangerously quivering lip. There's nothing like a non-sleeping, constantly breastfeeding baby, or a tantruming toddler to have people tutting your way.

Where, oh, where do we get these notions from, of good and

bad mothers? Good and bad children? But most of us have them. And they make us dance like puppets to their tune.

I tried, how I tried to do better, to be good. But then another baby was made.

And gradually the cords of my perfectionist self were cut – by sleepless nights, and heavy breasts, and tough decisions, and piercing wails. My dream of a perfect self has been unravelling fast. The sails of my soul unfurling, as I surrender to the winds of motherhood. And where I thought the sails of life should be stain-free and carefully pressed, I see that they are multi-colored and show the marks of storms they have weathered, the salt of tears cried and bleached by the sun. Their character comes from their imperfections.

There is nothing like the reality of three young children to wake you up to the fully rounded reality of yourself. Not what you wish you could be, but who you are, in your fullness – your compassion, your courage, your heart, your fierceness, your anger. . . we are all so much better than good or perfect could ever be.

And so this mothership is sailing into new waters. I am making peace with myself as I realize, what feels like a little too late: I am the perfect mother. . . for my children. And they are the perfect children. . . for me. We polish down each other's sharp corners, catch glimpses of our souls in each other's eyes. We hold each other in our frailties and in our celebrations. We shout in loud voices when our hearts are at a distance and whisper sweet words when our bodies are close. We stand together hand in hand. We grow together. Each imperfection a glistening facet in the diamonds of our ever-evolving selves.

This was my Dreaming Aloud column from JUNO magazine, Winter 2012.

caring

As mothers there's a lot of focus on caring. . .

Caring for your children, perhaps your partner, pets, garden. . . and other dependent family members too.

But what about yourself? To what extent do you care for yourself with the same love, energy and commitment?

Welcome to the circle

As mothers it is very easy to become subsumed into the whirlwind of daily life with children. Though we might yearn for time to ourselves, once we get it we don't know what to do with it, because we are not the same people we once were. I founded a women's group here in East Cork to answer this need in myself – we lasted for six years!

Our group of nine women met once a month at a different woman's house each time to simply take time out of being 'mum' and to reconnect to ourselves. This has been a lifeline for us all over the years, as we have helped each other through the death of close family members, new pregnancies, miscarriages, new motherhood, depression, frustrations at our partners and finding our own paths in life.

Welcome to the circle. Come in with your chatter, take off your coat. Find a place, slip off your shoes, wriggle your toes and tuck them under you.

The candle on the center table is lit. Its golden light softens the tired faces grouped around it. The brass singing bowl is sounded, its rich resonance dissipating into silence, leading us into the realm of stillness. We join hands and breathe together. In and out. This invisible trace leads us into ourselves. Conscious breath fills the room, sanctifying this simple lounge. Our separateness diminishes as a new energy enters the room tangibly changing the atmosphere: it is richer, heavier, and more somber. We settle deeper into stillness.

This is where we meet, on the first Sunday of every month. Although many of us meet at playgroup or for tea during the month, this is different. This is our space. Our sacred space in which we find ourselves once more.

We start, like always, by speaking to the very simple question:

"how are you really now?" In the stillness a small voice, which has been swamped by the busyness of daily mothering begins to emerge, haltingly, but with strength. How am I? How wonderful to be asked. Terrifying but wonderful. Can I speak to it, bring myself to this question with honesty? This is not a place for being 'fine'. No one here is interested in 'fine'. Here I can be confused, elated, barely scraping through. Here it is OK to inhabit a place of paradox or not knowing.

I start to speak, uncertain of where my words are headed. I surrender myself to them. Then, as I grab the thread more clearly I open my eyes and sweep them slowly around the room. Women who have become dear friends sit, their eyes focused and loving on me, as I unfold my soul before them. Not for approval, just to be witnessed, this tapestry of my life. The floor is mine, I cannot be interrupted. And it is such a wonderful feeling. Not to stop mid-sentence again and again to answer a child's question or grab a cup of juice from being spilt or pre-empt a sibling slap. Just space to be me. Wonderful.

And though mothering takes up so much of me, teaches me so much, satisfies me, there is also so much of me that is nothing to do with my kids, which has no expression in play dough or picture books or cooking dinner. The part of me from pre-kids, which inhabits dreams and books and philosophy. The part of me which even my husband does not really know and which I only get glimpses of. This gets a chance to creep out from under the stone of daily life and emerge blinking into the sunlight of awareness, to be witnessed by this circle of women. And then when another stands to speak I get to practice what I am so weak at in daily life, yet need for my parenting: deep, non-judgmental, open-hearted listening. This is where I learn skills which I take back home to my family.

Women's circles are as old as women themselves. At many times in history they have been outlawed, suspicious. At times they have held the names of quilting bees or sewing groups. Women's circles seem to be coming back, spreading like ripples through communities, sustaining the women who belong to them, their goodness spilling out into the families beyond.

We are not a great group of stitchers. Instead each month a different leader chooses a topic which stimulates our minds and titillates us: Creativity, Sex, Books, Community, Spirituality. . . But this is not a discussion group either, though the final discussions can be juicy. Instead we speak from our deepest selves in the spirit of council sharing, a custom borrowed from Native American elders, and familiar to me from Quaker meetings. Waiting for the spirit to move us, then allowing it to meander us through the topic. As we hear our voices speaking we discover what we truly feel and believe. Often it surprises the speaker herself. The listeners' heads nod in agreement, eyes well with tears of compassion. We sit in a circle and, as women, often we talk in circles too, round and round.

We drift out into the hallway, asking after our children's playmates, organising to meet up for coffee and playtime. We swap forgotten socks and disappear off into the night in time to fix supper for the family, or maybe, just perhaps, a little too late and so to be fed! I float into the house, transformed from the empty husk of a woman who left just a few hours before. I scoop up my children, delighting in their faces. "Mummy's back!" I announce, and I am. I really am.

This was my very first Dreaming Aloud column in JUNO magazine, Spring 2009.

How do you treat yourself?

How do you treat yourself?

By which I mean initially "what do you do to treat yourself?"

Chocolate, cakes, a night out, a shopping spree, a glass or three of wine?

But there is another layer to that question... How do you treat yourself?... meaning how do you *care* for you?

And a third layer which combines the two angles... how does *what* you do to *treat* yourself actually act to take care of you?

This is Big Stuff mamas.

Does what you do to celebrate or commiserate actually nourish your body? Does it fill your soul as well as your head or belly? Or does it make you sick or gain weight? Does it deplete your health or wealth?

So for example, cake has always been my treat of choice. The sugar gives me a lift. The wheat fills my belly. The fat makes me feel loved. The flavor tantalizes my taste buds. Cake means celebration. Sweetness is happiness. The act of sharing it (yes, sometimes I *do* share it, rather than wolfing it down by myself in the corner) adds communion to it.

But on another level the fat, sugar and wheat do *not* care for me. I get sugar highs... and lows. I crave it. Wheat bloats my belly horribly as I have an intolerance to it. And of course too much and I gain weight.

Chocolate is another big one for women. A way of treating themselves... which also leads to addiction, weight gain and sugar imbalances.

Or a drink or two of wine of an evening. Addiction... sugar imbalance...

For my kids it's sweets – candies, lollies... call them what you will. At one stage they were wanting them every day... until of their own volition (I *still* have no idea how it came about) they decided they'd have a Friday treat only. (They still have *way* more sugar than is good for them... but it was definitely a step in the right direction.)

Now let's take a moment and get clear on a few things:

- I am not taking a moral stance on sugar. There are many who condemn it as a poison and a drug. . .

- I love sugar. I love to bake, to make confectionary, desserts, cocktails. . .

- I am in no way a health freak. . . you can ask any of my friends and go through my kitchen cupboards.

- I am not trying to make you, or myself, or anyone feel guilty about it. Guilt doesn't work. It just tends to bite your butt. I'm all for abundance and feasting and pleasure with food.

- I am simply reflecting, mindfully, on my experiences and experiments with cutting down wheat and sugar in my own diet. . . after spending years resisting it.

Artificial sweetness

They feel good in the moment, these treats, they are rewards for getting through a day, achieving something, surviving. . . but in truth they are escape mechanisms, allowing us an "out" – through our bodies sure – but a way of not being here anymore. Because here is hard. It's just we're not supposed to feel that. So rather than dealing with overwhelm, rather than acknowledging how hard we are finding life, we treat ourselves. We sweeten the experience.

Listen up. If you're highly sensitive, if you have an addictive personality, if you self-medicate using food (*puts hand up*) then this is likely to be a major issue. Sweet pleasures to numb feelings and overwhelm. Being sensitive also means we are far more connected to the sensations in our bodies. We *feel* so much more and our emotions affect us physically, particularly in our gut. (which has more neurons than our brains apparently).

To protect ourselves we retreat into our minds, we distract

ourselves with comforts, we try to blend in and deny our nature.

We tend to be indulgent with easy sweetness. With cheap treats. The treats that do not really treat us.

Whilst at the same time thinking that the things that would truly nurture and nourish us are too expensive, too indulgent.

Treats used to be occasional. . . luxuries. But as life has gotten more complex and wearing on us mentally and emotionally. . . as we find ourselves giving more and more, becoming more overwhelmed. . . so treats have become more socially acceptable and affordable. We have become indulgent. We can counteract all the daily struggles, which take so much out of us (and which we usually deny are taking it out of us) by constantly rewarding ourselves. Like the reward charts that our children are bribed with at school. . . we're doing the same with ourselves.

What about if you re-learned to treat yourself? In a way that brings you more into connection with your body, with your soul, with those around you. How would that look and feel?

Authentic treats

We're talking authentic treats. Abundance that really nourishes us on every level. Stop snacking on, or binging on, artificial sweetness and cut yourself a slice of what you're really hungry for: connection, calm, physical pleasure, stillness, rest, authentic expression, time out, being held. . . You might find it in:

- an early night

- attending a women's circle

- meditating in the morning

- saying 'no' to the next request coming your way, with a big open loving heart

- a fresh fruit salad in the sun

- a long walk by yourself

- sitting with your journal and a steaming cup of tea

- snuggling up in front of the fire

- a massage – an orgasm – silence

- a hot bath

- reading poems aloud

- dinner with a loved one

- an e-course that nourishes you

- reading a special book

- a creative hour writing/ painting/ dancing/ sewing

That thing that you don't allow yourself. Can't allow yourself. . . because it's too indulgent. . . start with *that*. That thing you've been putting off, not getting round to. Especially if it doesn't cost a thing. Start with giving yourself permission to want it. Because pleasure in our culture is often seen as frivolous. Sinful. Wasteful. Unnecessary. And we believe we are unworthy of it.

And so we deny ourselves the pleasure we long for. . . and fill ourselves with something else more acceptable to our culture.

You are worthy of pleasure. The pleasure you long for.

You are valuable. There is nothing to prove. You do not need to earn it.

Your pleasure is of vital importance for your well-being. . . and the well-being of the world. Truly.

You want to help the world? Help yourself first. You want to make others feel good? Start by making yourself feel good. And it will bubble over. Out into the world.

It is not negative indulgence. It is positive. It is essential.

So allow it. So go on, give yourself permission to *enjoy* it. If it helps you absolutely have my permission to do it!

Fully treat yourself to some authentic sweetness. I dare you!

creativity

The greatest gift motherhood has given me is creativity.

It was during the latter stages of my first pregnancy that I touched my creativity for what seemed like the first time in years. I discovered a wonderful book, Birthing from Within, which used art therapy techniques as a form of birth preparation. And so I found myself 38 weeks pregnant, molding clay figurines. It was a surrendered state of creativity, the like of which I had not experienced since childhood.

This continued after my son's birth. But soon I found myself getting deeply frustrated: how could I honor my child's need for me, and my need to create?

I have lived this question for many years, through the birth of two more children, and the writing of books and painting of pictures by myself. As well as through drawing, puppet shows, singing, dancing and crafting alongside my children — my most treasured creations.

Creativity, the self-expression and celebration it brings, is at the heart of our family's life together and one of our greatest joys.

Creative renaissance and the womb

For uncountable generations of creative women the beginning of pregnancy meant the end of personal creativity. Once a woman's womb was filled with the life of another, her own creative life has been expected to end. A mother's job is to be a mother, she is told. Her creativity is a selfish vanity no longer required. It takes her away from the only job she should be doing: tending her family. If she refuses to give herself wholeheartedly to this, then she is classified a 'bad mother'.

Those who do not understand the renaissance that creative mothers experience try to reassure us and quiet down our fire. "You have all the time in the world to paint or write, babies are only young once," they counsel. They do not understand that this way madness and sadness lie. This is not just a whim which creative mothers need to put aside, but a biological reality.

The truth of the matter is that the creative mother who is unable to create, will not be a better mother, instead she is unable to mother properly either. Depression and despondency will pull her down, and the whole family with her. For the creative mother, creativity is her life force that makes her bloom. Take that from her and you take her soul.

This is where so many of us find ourselves. Lost and feeling alone, or even slightly mad: wanting to mother. . . and needing to create.

Introducing the Creative Rainbow Mother

I remember after a particularly bad day as a failed maternal angel and domestic goddess, I felt totally despondent. I knew that I just wasn't cut out for this mothering lark. I curled up in bed with another of my favorite books, Christiane Northrup's *Women's Bodies, Women's Wisdom*. I turned to the section on mothering and what I read was nothing short of a revelation to me:

I know that, beyond a doubt, I'm a Creative Rainbow Mother. I love to be alone. I love to read. I love quiet and music and writing. My soul is fed by long hours of unbroken creative time.

Somewhere deep inside a light went on, I totally connected with this other archetype of motherhood which she described in passing. I had never heard of it before, but felt it held the seed of myself. And so I avidly pursued this term, online and off. . . but there was not much about it anywhere.

Lynn V. Andrews, celebrated author and shaman, introduced the idea of the Creative Rainbow Woman in her third book, *Jaguar Woman.* In it she refers to the two mothering archetypes as the "Ecstatic Rainbow Mother" and the "Nurturing Earth Mother". The Rainbow Mother is often perceived, either in her own mind, or those of others, as a misfit. A dreamer and creatrix, she is always fluttering like a butterfly from one project to another, always trying new things. She regularly needs to descend into her creative depths, bringing visions between the physical world and the dream-time.

Whilst the Nurturing Mother finds immense comfort, safety and satisfaction in marriage, domesticity, growing food and children, and enjoys order around her, the Creative Rainbow Mother regularly feels the need to fly free. And the truth is that she is a divided soul. Her home and family, despite her great love for them, usually come second in her heart. Her spirit follows a different calling, often her art, but sometimes another career, which is, if she is honest with herself, the most important thing in her life. But she needs her home, her partner and children to help her to ground her energy and keep her in this world – and so there is a constant tension built into her relationships.

Intrigued by this discovery, seeing so many women that I shared it with lit up by it too, I wanted to find out: Why do some mothers need to create, as a matter of almost life and death? How can we empower this sort of woman? How can she find support and learn to support herself? What are the steps on the path which will transform her from lonely wanderer to fully fledged and fulfilled creative mother?

It is these questions and more that I could not find the answer to myself, as a new mother. There was nothing out there which even acknowledged the status of the creative mother, and her dilemmas, let alone looked into her biological, spiritual and practical needs. It was a journey that would transform my life, and find form in a book: *The Rainbow Way: cultivating creativity in the midst of Motherhood*, which has been transforming the lives of the creative mothers who have since read it. There are now groups – online and on the ground – inspired by it, creative businesses and careers started because of it. I am both delighted and honored that it has found such a passionate readership.

Renaissance

Many of the women I spoke to in the research for the book, experienced a rebirth of themselves as both women and creatives when they became mothers. It is something they were neither prepared for, nor knew how to handle. Because no one spoke about it. And so they felt alone, confused and unsupported. Overwhelmed by the dual strength of their maternal and creative drives. Each as powerful as the other. Each requiring her heart, soul and total dedication.

I believe that the word renaissance perfectly describes the experience of many creative mothers. From "re-" meaning again, and "naissance" meaning birth, it speaks of the fact that through pregnancy, birth, and motherhood, women find themselves "born again". For many this is an instantaneous life-altering shift, and felt as a spiritual experience. For others it is a growing sense of realization that "something profound has changed in my life: I am no longer who I once thought I was".

It is as though the vital forces which have been ignited in our bodies through pregnancy and birth also rekindle our creative passion. It seems that a woman's body does not differentiate between the biological and artistic acts of creation, they are fuelled by the same fire and cultivated under the same conditions: our womb is our crucible of creativity.

The womb: crucible of creativity

For many women pregnancy is the first time their womb has been 'activated'. Perhaps a lifetime of unfulfilling sexual encounters, or a sense of disconnection from their menstrual cycle, means that their womb has been a part of their body which has been ignored or even despised. Now, called into life through the act of pregnancy, the latent energies within are activated. Hence the sudden 'switching on' of creativity. For the first time in their adult lives, women's eyes are opened to their ability to nurture life, to create, and their hormones are moving them into the perfect level of consciousness to do just this.

Whereas before getting into this creative state would require willpower and dedication, now her hormones and activated womb magically smooth the way. The pregnant woman finds that she is no longer in control of her own body's processes in a way she previously believed. She is now surrendered to them. Her logical brain, which has been honed by her education, and her body which has previously competed on a male stage, are now flooded with feminine creative powers. To find pleasure and comfort, to make some sort of sense of these new experiences. A woman who has previously been taught to express herself creatively, will often turn to these skills as a way to express these new feelings, powerful dreams, strange longings and disorienting physical changes that she is experiencing.

The creative renaissance in new mothers is, I believe, the result of an incredibly complex, once-in-a-lifetime shift of the woman's hormonal, emotional, physical and psychological states, along with a total shift in her social role, responsibilities and daily routine. It is something which has not been researched, and so I can only begin to put together the pieces.

For women who have learnt ways of tapping into their creativity, who know how to tune into this subterranean stream of images and ideas which slip below the radar of the conscious mind, the coupling of increased creative brain activity (increased alpha and theta waves), powerful emotions, an awakening of forgotten memories and dreams, heightened intuition, decreased physical activity and raised hormone levels, and added blood flow to the womb and vaginal area, place her in the biologically optimal state for creative flow.

For such a common experience, you will find little said about it. It is not a topic which is well-funded, or of great interest to most (male) research scientists. And so each woman in our culture tends to experience this transformation and renaissance by herself, with little guidance or preparation. Then, having had the experience, thinks that she is alone in it and either ignores or dismisses it as she has no frame of reference for it. As a culture we do not acknowledge what a massive shift becoming a mother is for any woman, let alone explore this creative renaissance that so many women experience. It is my deepest desire to help to prepare and initiate women, because without guidance and support a woman can feel alone, misunderstood, or just plain 'wrong' in her experiences, which her doctor, friends and partner have no understanding of.

A woman's soul journey is integral to the creative journey: any woman who embarks wholeheartedly on one, often unwittingly embarks on the other. This is the crux of being a Creative Rainbow Mother. It is more than how many jumpers you have knitted, or having an exhibition in a fancy gallery, or a bookshelf of your own books: it is about the act of living authentically whilst honoring your mother self and creative self. About saying yes to life, every part of your life.

A shorter version of this article first appeared in The Mother magazine, Nov/Dec 2013.

Dancing

The sun is shining. "Let's go out for a walk," I suggest.

"Don't wanna go out, Mum!" my older daughter insists.

"We can go and see the chickens, and the pigs," I wheedle.

"Don't wanna go!" The tone is being ramped up. I cannot face another tantrum. We have been through too many these past few days. My nerves are raw. But still we have been cooped up in the house for weeks with illness. I need to get some exercise. I need to move my body, get my heart pumping, tone my muscles, feel alive. And then the penny drops. I go over to the stereo in the children's room. It is used solely for story tapes and lullabies. I put on Bruce Springsteen's glorious folksy *Seeger Sessions*. I love this CD. My kids love this CD. It just has to be danced to.

And I start to dance. Awkwardly at first, self-conscious of the audience of two little girls, a creaky mama body that doesn't move quite as easily as it used to, and a pair of enormous breasts that move too independently for my liking.

I keep glancing out the window to see if the neighbors are watching. I start with some line dancing. The charleston. Then a little belly dancing. Then some aerobics. All the dances and moves from different times in my life. And then full flung mad skipping, whirling and swirling until my heart is racing. The baby is jigging up and down on her bum, clapping in delight. I clap back and wave my arms in the air like I just don't care. My two-year-old, who has refused to change her clothes/pajamas for three days, grabs her dress off the shelf – in her eyes you *have* to wear a dress for dancing. She has seen mama dancing enough times to know that skirts (which this mama lives in) swirl wonderfully out when dancing.

And so we dance together, whirling and spinning, and swinging her and flying her onto the bed. Her eyes sparkle with delight, cheeks flushed. "Again, mama, again!" Oh, how I loved that too when I was a little girl, my father would put on his rock and roll records and we would jive and then he would fly me through the air. The feeling of freedom from gravity. Breathless exhilaration. Pure physical joy. Again, again!

We dance with teddies, run in circles, freeze between songs, bring out the tambourines, until at last we collapse on the bed, our hearts racing, grins on our sweaty faces. Happy dancing girls!

Sleep

Who knew that sleep would be such a big deal?

But when you have children it becomes your guiding compass. . . how much sleep you have dictates the tone and mood of the day. Nap times become the Holy Grail. Relationships falter over the trench warfare between those who advocate differing styles of sleep: cot or co-sleeping, controlled crying or comfort.

Adventures without sleep

I was blessed with three non-sleeping children, who lulled us into a false sense of security as infants, only to transform in to multiple night-waking babies from the age of three months to two years. I cannot begin to express the levels of sleep deprivation under which I have functioned for almost seven years straight.

Whoever coined the phrase "sleeping like a baby" was not, I would bet, a parent. Of course, there are some who are blessed with wonder-babies who sleep through the night from the beginning. But for the rest of us sleep is, at some stage in the first few years of a child's life, a major issue.

Well-meaning loved ones and medical professionals shower you with suggestions, most commonly: stop breastfeeding, put them in their own bed and the worst, and just let them cry it out.

Let me share our story. . .

My son Timmy certainly prepared me for the time ahead before he was even born. I remember lying awake whilst he tumbled about inside me like a circus acrobat until his self-appointed bedtime of 1.30am and not a moment sooner! Then whilst he had a lie in, I was up at 6am for work! And so this timetable continued after his gentle birth at home.

I have some friends who didn't know what to do with themselves in the first few weeks of their newborns' lives as they slept all the time. No such joy for me. My son fed all the time, and could sleep for long times at a stretch – as long as he was in my arms. However, the second I put him down to go to the toilet, or get feeling back into my dead arm, my peaceful child would scream as though possessed.

Whilst daytime sleep was almost non-existent – just half an hour here or there, he knew night from day, and by two weeks old had slept through the night. I was delighted. I was a good parent. I was in control. And so this continued until he was four months old, sleeping through more nights than he didn't. Then, what started as an innocent sniffle turned into a severe cold, my life turned upside down.

My once sleeping baby, who had happily graduated to a crib beside our bed, was not only back in bed with us, but on the breast all night. Any time his mouth became detached from the nipple he would wake with a scream. He was snuffling and feverish: I felt desperately sorry for him. But days later when the cold had subsided his sleeping was just the same. After two weeks of this my nerves were raw, eyes so tired I couldn't keep them open.

Christmas came; I was on my knees after a month of wakings every forty minutes from midnight till six, sometimes every twenty minutes. When asked what I wanted for Christmas my heartfelt request was a decent night's sleep. And yet that was the one thing no one could give me. He was a joy to me most of the time, but at night I was at my wits end.

Boxing Day came, no sleep for Christmas and another cold. My previous lack of sleep seemed luxurious. Now I was awake for three hours straight from 2-5am as well as multiple other wakings. After that I banned any clocks from the bedroom, each night became a blur of waking and dozing.

I begged friends, family, child care professionals for tips – I tried them all. Older locals rolled their eyes as I recounted how, not only was he not sleeping through the night, but also he was waking fifteen plus times. The 'rod for your own back speech' was rolled out. What sort of a mother was I for not letting him cry it out rather than martyr myself? And so after two months I gave in and tried. He cried for 45 minutes, despite my going in at intervals to reassure him, then vomited all over himself, his whole body shaking – I felt sick to my stomach – my exhaustion had led me to do something I swore I never would, and my husband and I vowed to the bottom of our hearts that we never would do again. To this day I still feel sick thinking about it, it is my absolute parenting low point.

Over the next couple of months we tried putting him back in his own crib, having him in the bed with us, moving our whole family onto futons in front of the fire in the sitting room. We tried earlier and later bedtimes, not breastfeeding to sleep, a musical box, bath time before bed, soothers and bottles, teddies and lovies – all to no avail.

Friends and family were supportive, incredulous that I was still surviving on so little sleep. But few had experienced night-waking to this degree and so did not truly understand the level of exhaustion I felt. My mother used to say sleep deprivation was a form of torture and whilst she was right, turning myself into the victim and my son the perpetrator did not help in any way. Instead I had to develop my compassion for him and myself, my resilience and acceptance of the situation. There were days when I was too tired to be safe to drive, many we curled up on the sofa in front of daytime TV. We went to friends' houses where I would eat, cry and be comforted.

My waking moments were spent searching for answers. *The Science of Parenting* and *The No Cry Sleep Solution* confirmed my worries about leaving children to cry it out and were supportive of my approach. *Night-time Parenting* by William and Martha Sears was compassionate too. "Nightwaking", they explained "has survival benefits. In the first few months, babies' needs are the highest, but their ability to communicate their needs is the lowest." It explained that our societies' expectation that babies sleep through the night was unrealistic and that just because it was night time didn't mean you stopped being a parent. Which was fine. But sleep had become the be all and end all of my life, dominating my thoughts, day and night.

I was looking for an answer. Any answer. And in the end the

only answer was time. If you had told me then that I would continue this way for another year. I would not have believed it was possible. If you told me it would happen just the same with another two babies my jaw would have hit the floor.

But it did. And we all, somehow, lived to tell the tale. But answers – they were in short supply.

A version of this article was first published in Modern Mum magazine.

Routine and rhythm

This seems to be one of the biggest issues of motherhood – do you have your baby in a routine? Baby-led mothering versus routine-based is a big divider in our culture.

"Have you got that baby into a routine yet?"

My skin crawls at that question. I object to it on so many levels: have I imposed my way of being onto my baby? Do we live a fixed pattern dictated by someone else? No, no, no! But we've got rhythm!

I like to be free, yet I live in a world that values order and structure. I am not a regular person and my son was not a standard issue baby; I am not sure how many people are. And yet so much of what is offered as guidance to new parents asks them to abandon their own instincts or observations and follow a fail-proof, step-by-step plan to success written by an expert. It's scientific, so it must be good, mustn't it? You must have a routine, otherwise... Otherwise what? Otherwise you'll have to think for yourself?

When I started out on the mothering road I didn't go near the infamous *Contented Little Baby* book or anything else remotely similar: it went totally against my own nature to be that rigidly structured. I needed guidance, not a timetable. I like flexibility, the opportunity to see what each day presents me with and the chance to adapt to and integrate that, not ignore it because NOW and no other time is nap-time.

And then reality hit this idealist square in the face. It took me by my hair and shook me awake, every night, in the form of a waking baby. My little boy who until four months old had reveled in flexibility, suddenly began waking multiple times a night – and continued doing so, night after night, week after week, month after month. Muddle-headed from exhaustion, I had to re-evaluate. I was forced to confront this resistance to routine and its implications in my own life. Reflection led me to see that my son seemed to be literally crying out for more rhythm to our lives so that he could orientate himself in space and time. It was on reading two wonderful books that I began to create more balance in both our lives. Rahina Baldwin's *You Are Your Child's First Teacher* and Elizabeth Pantley's *No-Cry Sleep Solution* brought home to me the importance of helping your child to establish rhythm in their day. It has been a powerful learning curve for me understanding the difference between routine and rhythm and the difference between guiding and imposing structure on your children. But is that just playing with words, I hear you ask, and what is the difference anyway?

I would define a routine as a schedule which is set externally, usually based on external authority or advice. Especially popular in the last 50 years or so have been scientific routines based (supposedly) on objective scientific fact, rational and impersonal: babies should be fed every four hours, sleep in a crib and drink eight fluid ounces of carefully balanced formula milk, wean at four or six months and not before or much after, potty train at 18 months, bed at 7pm etc. These systems were devised for an average baby, whom I have yet to meet. They are based on the judgments of others and the fashions of the time. They do not take into account the individual's idiosyncrasies, physical build, character type and living environment. They are a one-size-fits-all blueprint into which the individual must fit himself.

Rhythms on the other hand reflect and are propelled by nature: breathing in and out, eating and defecating, sleeping and waking, menstruation, the rising and setting of the sun and moon, the changing seasons, the passing of years. Each has its own ebb and flow; they are not static. To take just one example, menstruation, whilst often 28 days, is affected by stress or the hormones of other women that we are close to, and so is rarely precise in its arrival. Our own nature is rooted in its own internal rhythms and immersed in an external world of nature's rhythms.

Humans need rhythm to function healthily and achieve balance, indeed this is the basic principle behind many philosophies of health such as acupuncture or homeopathy, in biology it is known as homeostasis. Rhythm can be defined as a self-regulating system which fluctuates, tending towards equilibrium because of the constant feedback received from both itself and its environment. Routine, on the other hand, is pre-designated, man-made and arbitrary. Rather than seeing daily life as a set of alienated actions all requiring precision, as routine dictates, a rhythmic approach encourages us to look holistically at our days and the patterns woven into them by our basic physical needs and other activities requiring balance. It is the difference between creating an original piece of art and following a paint by numbers: one takes more thought and effort, but the result is infinitely more rewarding.

This article was first published in Modern Mum magazine.

Shared sleep

You are there to greet me when I crawl into bed, willing the covers to be silent as I pull them over us. Your moth breath, your long lashes on cream cheeks, hands curled into soft chubby fists. My heart is still. . . and pounding at the same time with love, with gratitude for this magic. Almost every night for six years I have come to bed to this sight, I have woken to this sight. . . different little people, same sight, and I will never tire of it.

Your body snuggles close into mine when you discover that I am here, we complete each other. You whimper, turning your head towards me, mouth like a fish. Your eyelids flicking open. You connect to my breast, the look of pure ecstasy flutters them closed again. You suck contentedly to sleep, to dreams I will never know behind your spider eyes. We will continue this dance all night – coming together, pulling apart. I remember when first I did this with your brother, I struggled with the endless, hourly, half hourly imposition on my right to sleep, now I drift in and out, a seasoned pro. The waves of slumber never far from my shores, I bob in semi consciousness all night, and wake half refreshed. At times you writhe and moan and need more than I can give. I feel sucked dry, no liquid gold left to give. And so I place you on my chest, ear to my heart. You nuzzle into me. We are complete once more.

I could not imagine you in a crib, cold and alone. This is where my babies need to be. Where I need them. Snuggled up warm and close. It is a primal need. The bonds of love cannot stretch through to another room. They are too short still. But one day they will lengthen and the need for sleep will finally override the need for togetherness. We will both feel able to stretch the cord further.

How can people worry about this intimacy? I am no more likely to make love to you than to a cat or dog. Yet people share their beds with those pets. I will caress your chubby thighs, marvel at your lashes, and breathe in your sweet breath. But nothing more. I am your mama, you are safe with me. Nor will I roll over you or smother you – you are not a doll. Even on your first day of life you and I knew each other. We talked cell to cell, eye to eye, skin to skin, heart to heart. Aware of the others' presence or absence with every fiber of our beings.

We share our cocoon of love as the morning wears on and the sun gets higher. Into this warm den come older babies for their dose of snuggle love. It is this which makes them grow. And this which soothes my soul. My precious snuggly babies. I feel the sand slipping though my fingers. Our shared sleeping nights are numbered, their preciousness disappearing with your puppy fat and baby curls, my mother heart aches for them already – I hold you a little closer and wish.

Are you a morning goddess?

How do you start your morning?

I know that how I start mine sets the tone for my day. A few moments mindful breathing and I am a far nicer mama. Hassle and whinge and jump on me and I'm set to banshee mode for the rest of the morning. How we start the day matters. But as mamas often this is outside of our control. All these wonderful self-help books tell you to do an hour's yoga and half an hour's meditation followed by an unharried breakfast of fruit. But they don't have little kids.

When trying not to put your knickers over your tights, (or even to find clean knickers in the laundry mountain!) is an issue. Clean clothes and a shower are major achievements worthy of a Nobel Prize.

When rather than choosing to rise earlier you are begging for another second of shuteye after a night of constant wakings and wriggly children coughing in your face or wetting the bed next to you.

Sometimes it feels that you are defeated before the day has even begun. Especially if you are parenting single handed.

But if you can find a way to have five minutes peace, and some sort of mindfulness practice – be it yoga, a walk in the garden, a jot in your journal. . . whatever little hit of headspace, body awakening and peace you can to carry into your day with you, then take it, dear mama, you will all be better for it.

Nourish yourself dear mama, water your soul with silence, and honor your body with love.

I don't want to go to bed

I don't want to go to bed.

This is what my children say at the end of a long, tiring day.

But now I find myself there too. Having a mummy tantrum.

I don't want to go to bed. Because going to bed means putting myself away. Giving myself up. Giving up.

Sure as night follows day another morning will be there to greet me when I open my eyes. Another morning of fighting and whinging and sandwich-making, dishwasher-stacking, breastfeeding, uniform-finding. And really I haven't the heart.

I am tired. Tired of being nice. Of making peace. Of worrying that I am being good enough. Of being told I'm not.

Tired of food and dishes and cleaning.

It is one minute off midnight. I should be in bed. I will be tired for another endless day. Which only makes it worse. But I cannot bring myself to go.

I want to stay here forever.

In the quiet of this house. Curled up and writing. My thoughts, my own. My body, my own.

Nobody wants me now. Nobody needs me.

I am just me. I am free to think, to write, to move. And the silence so thick that the fish tank sounds as loud as a waterfall.

I am me. Not somebody else's help-meet. Just me.

Here I am not failing at discipline, worrying about how to get a child to eat or shit, making more food which will be rejected, concerned as to whether my behavior will scar them for life or make my husband leave, wondering how much more TV is acceptable to have on, having to answer the same question for the 50th time, feigning interest in Lego models or sympathy for a puny scratch, or worrying about someone seeing the state of the house.

My day is filled with these things and they bore me with their monotony. When where I really want to be is here. Just me and my thoughts and a computer. Me and a book. In silence.

I spend my days hungry for this time. I feel guilty that I take it, perched in front of my screen, knowing I should be nice to my husband, talk to him, and show an interest.

But I just want to be me… just for a moment to feel myself more fully, to have a thought that isn't interrupted, and to do something that is of value. To matter to myself… and the world beyond these four walls.

To be valued. Oh, to be valued.

The motherload is very hard sometimes. Especially at the stroke before midnight.

I don't want to go to bed.

Embracing change

The journey of motherhood from its first moments, is one of learning to embrace change: changing moods, ever-growing children, our changing bodies during pregnancy. . .

In transition

Before enlightenment chop wood, carry water.
After enlightenment chop wood, carry water.

Traditional Buddhist saying

In the moment of enlightenment nothing changes but perception.

Just like nothing changes between your body being pregnant and your mind knowing that you are. Nothing. Except everything does change. Even third time round. It is a paradigm shift of the first degree every time – the magician pulls the rug from under your previous plans and vision of reality and shows you a gaping hole of the unknown and unknowable tunneling nearly eighty years hence. "Will you ride the rollercoaster?" he asks – but the question has already been answered. The question mark now lies safely buried in my womb, growing bigger by the hour. What is pregnancy, birth and parenting but a never-ending lesson in surrender to constant change? And I am a slow learner. I drag my heels and want to be in charge, to know what's happening, to plan and control.

Perhaps it is not the conception of a child for you, but the death of a loved one, the end of a relationship, the loss of a job, a life changing realization, a change in health, moving homes or even countries. Transitions are often unanticipated, at least by the conscious mind. Unpredictable and unknowable, they change our perception of everything which we class as ours, shaking the apparent solidity of ego. A major transition reveals the nature of reality as being in constant flux, and out of our ultimate control. In his insightful book *Transitions*, William Bridges notes the three stages integral to transition are an ending, followed by a period of crisis and confusion, followed by a new beginning. By nature we humans are not much good at endings.

Major transitions can often spark paradigm shifts. It is as

though someone has removed a veil from your eyes, and shown you that what you previously took to be reality is actually an illusion. Suddenly you awaken to a totally different level of understanding, as though your eyes have been opened, where once you were sleep-walking. The world is made anew seen from this altered perspective.

The term 'paradigm shift' was first used by Thomas Kuhn, a science historian and philosopher in his 1962 book, *The Structure of Scientific Revolutions*. A paradigm (from the Greek *paradigma*, 'pattern') is a framework of thought, a scheme for understanding and explaining certain aspects of reality. A paradigm shift is not more knowledge but a new knowing, a transformation of our perceptual matrix.

Marilyn Ferguson, author of the ground-breaking *Aquarian Conspiracy*, (my personal 'desert island' book, which I have read and re-read countless times), wisely counsels: "you can't embrace the new paradigm unless you let go of the old. Like the gestalt switch, it must occur all at once. The new paradigm is not 'figured out' but suddenly seen."

This is what radical thinkers have been arguing, for decades, must happen to our culture to transform and survive. And it is happening. Now. The credit crunch, banking crash, expenses scandals, swine flu and Ebola have started a paradigm shift in many who previously truly believed in the reality and rightness of our system.

A paradigm shift is really the exposure of thought and belief as just that, dry shells, not reality. The discarded chrysalis of an old way of being, they can neither contain nor sustain us, however much we wish for the comfort of the familiar, with its attendant clarity and simplicity. We have inexorably entered a new level of awareness, a new way of being, with greater complexity and potentially a higher level of integration. But in order to enter that place first we must venture through no-man's land: a place of chaos and uncertainty which tests us to the limits, where the old rules don't work and the new rules have yet to be made. This liminal state of being is the first trimester of pregnancy, the transition phase of labor, the first few weeks after birth. It is the state we are now in in our world.

This cracking of the cosmic egg allows for new life, new creativity, new potential – but its chasm is so conceptually far from our previous ground that we cannot leap it with our minds. Just as any birth-mother knows, that you cannot give birth with your mind alone, however much you wish it. We must do it emotionally and spiritually naked. How exhilarating and terrifying, this vast seamlessness of possibility. "Who am I? How can it be?" we call our questions to the wind and our voice echoes back unanswered. The pieces shift around us. And then just as we despair of surviving, the mandala comes into view: in a word, an image, a phrase, a face, a glimpse of one part, but it is enough. The transition has been made. A new world awaits. . .

This was my Dreaming Aloud column from JUNO magazine, Winter 2009.

Milestones

We are told as parents that there is an invisible line, which we are always looking out for. The first times. The big achievements. The milestones: the first word, the first step. . . These concrete proofs of our children's steps into individuality. There are myriad baby journals sold to record these momentous occasions which stack up in the first two years of life.

This subject of milestones has been pertinent to me over these past months as my youngest learns to communicate with words and actions, to play with us, to build towers and dig the earth.

And as my oldest learns to ride a bike and swim, and my middle child learns to draw recognizable images and had her first day at playschool.

I find myself wanting to keep her first 'real' picture, but looked at in the flow of all her other pictures it is less clear-cut than this. In this one there are eyes and a mouth, in that one eyes and hair. This one is what she says is a crocodile, but this one really looks like a crocodile. And so I keep them all, because they show the process of growth, of development: up and down, back and forwards.

A friend's baby is learning to walk. Holding her hands he places one foot in front of the other, then lets go: one hand, then the other. He wobbles, and squidges onto his padded bum. But for a moment he was standing on his own two feet. For the first time. He beams in delight.

We strengthen our muscles, arrange our neurons, observe, absorb. . . and then one day. . . we can! We just can.

But before we do it for the world to see, our ability to do it is there. We can walk before we can walk. We are simply waiting for the courage to try, the belief that we can, building our trust in the world and ourselves.

So to focus solely on the milestones, means we take our eye off all the unseen work that goes on before, or the perfecting that goes on after: the honing and refining of these skills, the failures and frustrations. These are not considered 'the real thing' or part of it. We only focus on the success. On the 'moments' – the wedding not the marriage, the birth and not the mothering of a newborn. These are what we are told to value. The milestone events that can be sold to us, the tangible achievements in what is a murky river of learning and life, scattered with learning on all different levels all of the time.

I know when I judge my mothering on the milestone moments alone, there are times when I would most definitely 'fail'. True, some days I might win awards for patience or creativity, but many others I miserably fail. When really neither are true. The whole thing is a learning process, feedback, adjustment, reflection, trial and error. No one on the outside sees the cogs whirring in my head, nor do they see when something is natural and instinctive. The same is so true of our children learning to be little functioning humans.

This is why I keep my own journals. I think I am always getting 'better' and scorn my younger 'naive' self, after all that's what our culture teaches us about history. But then I look back and see what my twenty-five-year-old-new-mother-self 'knew' that I have now forgotten, or am just re-discovering. The path of learning is filled with many levels, some visible, some invisible, and we move between them, sometimes manifesting our knowledge clearly, demonstrating what we know, and at others times we seem to be 'stuck' or regressing, yet learning is happening.

It all counts. Not just the milestones but the tantrums, the scribbles, the mess. They are just evidence of the wonderful muddled journey of learning that we are all on. Oh, how much more we can all do than we show right now. It's all there, bubbling, just below the surface. We just have to keep believing.

This was a Dreaming Aloud column from JUNO magazine.

Learning to fly

Have you ever watched a butterfly be born?

We did, over breakfast. It is the sort of moment that you get to experience with children, which, in the adult world would most probably pass you by. An everyday miracle.

We had been feeding the caterpillars fresh green leaves every day for almost two weeks. Watched as they'd crawled in procession to the top of the cage, and then woke one morning to find them all suspended upside down from silken threads. Dangling precariously. Their once soft green bodies now hard and brown.

And then nothing. For days and days. We began to grow impatient.

They had been in their chrysalises so long we were starting to think they were dead.

Change it seems takes time.

So this morning, as we were eating breakfast, I notice a butterfly.

Just one.

We all crowded around the cage, watching the chrysalises for signs of life. And then another emerges. And another.

Leaving their old skins behind – brittle and transparent – they stand, still, carefully, wings still wet from the imaginal soup. Like spring leaves they unfurl. Stillness subsides into tiny tremors, then bigger shaking, and finally flutters. Slowly, slowly the caterpillar is feeling into its new form.

And as the wings get bigger and flatter, stillness reigns once more.

Later in the day we open the cage. It is full of butterflies which had hatched earlier in the day. They are crawling up and down the net.

We blow at one which is perched at the top of the cage. Nothing between it and freedom but a flap of its wings. It resists. I poke its legs gently. It kicks back.

Another first – being kicked by a butterfly!

The children don't believe me, so try it themselves. The butterfly kicks them too.

And then it just stands there.

"Why isn't it flying?" The children want to know. The neighboring children have joined us too at this stage. All gathered around in awestruck delight at this tame, newborn butterfly.

"Because it doesn't know it can," I reply, "it never has before, and it has no reason to think it can now. It probably still thinks it's a caterpillar, because that's what it's always been. Only we can see it's a butterfly."

Suddenly, a small gust of wind unsettles it. It flaps. . . and flies. . . only a few halting flaps. . . and onto a child's hair!

A little nudge and up it goes again. . . Up, up, up into the blue sky. . . you could almost hear its tiny butterfly voice – "I can fly. I can *fly!*" We watched in delight as it disappeared into the blue.

We think of butterflies as free. . . but in fact when they are newborn, they are cautious. They cling. Earth-bound.

Just like us.

And. . . you know the twist in the tale, the moral of the story that I'm getting out, dear mama? That's right! You aren't the little grub you thought you were. . . you can fly. . .

So why not test those wings?

Baby steps and belief

Our fourteen-month-old keeps letting on that she can talk. "Hi Daddy!" she says this week, it just slips out. . . we are all amazed. And then she goes silent. "What was that?" we ask each other.

Another day we are reading together "Book!" she exclaims, then silence once more.

Before we speak, before we know that we can speak, before others hear what we have to say, we first have to believe that we have something that we want to communicate.

That first word is a leap of faith. . . Even though we have never done it before, we cannot do it without... doing it. We have absorbed our mother tongue, we have learnt to shape our mouths, to vibrate our vocal chords with ever more complex gurgles and whoops. And then, one day, we decide to try. "Yes!" We have birthed our first word.

We are simply waiting for the courage to try, the belief that we can, building our trust in the world and ourselves. Only the baby can decide to speak, no one can do it for her. It is a leap of faith. Fuelled by deep desire to play a more equal part in the workings of the world, to communicate, to be heard, to be known, to join in.

Same goes for you!

You might be wanting to be an artist, or a writer, or a mother, or speak a new language, and can't see how it's going to happen, how to start, how to do it...

But you have it within you, just there below the surface, this latent potential, unknown and unseen – water it, feed it, and then one day let the bird of your talent fly free.

Life, in all its guises is really about getting your hands dirty rather than holding yourself back because you're worried about mucking up... it is a leap of faith.

It is by doing, not thinking, that we become. We can get so caught up in our minds, in having to be perfect before we will even try. But we have to be prepared to fall... in order to be able to fly.

What's the worst that can happen?

Birth that baby, that book, that painting... All you have to do is believe it... and start it! One baby step at a time, birth yourself into the world.

We need you and your talents. Your offerings. Your gifts.

love

Love is at the heart of motherhood. But it is not quite as straight forward and fluffy as the movies would have us believe. Some of us are good at expressing it (and I would most definitely put myself in that camp). Others struggle to express it. But it is there.

More than the whole world

My four-year-old daughter tells me she loves me multiple times a day. At night this little girl, who never used to like kisses or cuddles at all, now snuggles in close, kisses me on the lips. And so begins our little ritual.

"I love you, Mummy!"

"I love you too, sweetness!"

"I love you more than you love me!" she asserts. I feel a little sad, it's probably true. Her heart is so big, so open.

"But I love you more than chocolate!" (This, I am sad to say is a maternal white lie, though at moments like this it is most definitely true).

"But I love you more than everything in the whole wide world!"

And she means it. And I'm a schmuck who really doesn't deserve it. The pure innocence of love. I drink it up and silently promise to do better, to be a little more deserving of this radiant, be-dimpled, golden-haired love.

The matador

"I love you, Mummy," she whispers in the dark. Warm body curled into mine.

I am the matador. She the bull. We have danced our dance. Her horns, my red cape. Swirling, skidding, almost colliding, side-stepping. The chance of a goring always close.

Ten minutes earlier a scream in the dark. Full throated. A mama who had reached the end of a very long tether, of side-stepping and distracting this bull child who has been needling for a fight for days. Like seeding rain clouds she finds some inner relief in it, it seems.

But it is exhausting, this battle of wills and patience.

It has taken every tactic I know to keep a smile on my face and the show on the road. We have had not a threat, nor a raised voice from the matador. Tights have been adjusted and readjusted for half an hour at a time. Every morning. And blankets. Multiple times. Every night. And everything else has been done and redone for her. Until finally, and suddenly, red. Enough. Scream.

The horns were there ready to gore me. My weakness finally exposed. "You hate your children," her voice crows, triumphant. No, no, no I don't, I say inside and out. Just this matador's body and brain are tired. There is no more fight, nor patience left in me.

A retreat. I am followed. An explanation. And back into bed. Together. In stony silence and blackness. Broken by a kiss. "I love you, Mummy," she says.

Tender

A reader responded to the previous piece of writing:

"I know this scene! We can do that dance. Just last night. Afterwards my daughter made me a card, carefully cut out with colored in love hearts and best handwriting "To Mum, Mum loves me, I love Mum" (oh!) and sweet words, connection, understanding. This love is so huge."

On reading her response it occurred to me – maybe the fight beforehand is a way of tenderizing us, like the way we bash meat with a mallet to make it less tough.

Perhaps anger, battles and even hate are the best way the Universe knows of opening us fully to love. Of taking away our defenses, leaving us standing there vulnerable and open so that love can just pour in. So that we can really feel it to the tips of our toes, really feel how big and true it is, so that we can, even if just for a moment, have our entire beings taken over by love, and feel the most profound connection – made even more special by knowing how it feels to be absent from it and have come so close to losing it.

Imagine.

I think it might just be true!

And if it is, it means that everything that comes between us is just interference in the bandwidth of pure love flowing between us all.

What's love got to do with it?

Perhaps I was letting myself in for it. But you see, I couldn't help myself! I wanted to hear it from their own little mouths. I wanted to hear how treasured and adored and all round lovely this exhausted mama was. Just to make it all worthwhile. I had just witnessed a friend's child break off from playing to come and tell her mum how much she loved her. I tell my kids how much I love them so frequently that my son says, "I know that, you tell us all the time", his tone of voice says, *Duh! Tell me something I don't know!*

So I ask, sure of the response. "Do you love Mummy?"

"No!" comes the answer from the three-year-old. "But I love the baby"... this is the baby who she tried to push down the stairs only minutes earlier, who, on a daily basis is slapped, throttled, pushed, pinched and bitten.

"Oh! Are you sure?" I wheedle. Never particularly endearing, begging to be loved by your children. . .

"No," she asserts "because you're stupid!"

Ah, great, wasn't expecting that! Ego definitely deflated now!

"What about you?" I ask my five-year-old. "Do you love Mummy?"

"No!" he says.

He was my safe bet, my affectionate little boy. "Are you sure?"

He thinks long and hard, looking at my face. One thumb goes up, the other down. "Sometimes yes, sometimes no."

OK, we're getting somewhere. "When don't you love me?"

"When you don't let me watch TV or when I want to play Lego and you say we have to go out. . ."

"And when do you?" he lists the opposite.

"So you loving me is about what I do?" He nods. How unconditional, I think sarcastically. . . But then I think of my own feelings. I feel love for my children when they are doing what I want, I don't feel it at all when they are screaming, rude, demanding, mean. I feel love for my husband when he brings me breakfast in bed or says I look nice, I don't feel it when he hasn't done the washing up and it's his turn, or when he is home late. . . oh, whoops, so much for my mature, developed unconditional love.

I ask my daughter again. This time she says. . . "No. But I'll love you when I'm bigger, when I'm big like you."

Oh how true, little wise one, it is only now, having put to bed most of my disgruntledness about my less-than-perfect parents who didn't do this and did do the other that I didn't like, that I am really beginning to love them. . .

I see that we use love as a currency, as a bribe, a manipulator, a currency, an ego booster. . . "Do you love me?" We want to know. . . please make me feel special, feel alright. "I'll love you, if you love me" we trade with our kids and partners. We say it in the flush of passion, in the darkness of the night. But what, really, does it mean?

I need you, I want you, I feel lost without you, I'm happy, I'm excited, I'm grateful, I'm scared I might lose you. . . all these things and more. We use "I love you" to bind others to us. . . but the old saying is true: "If you love someone, let them go, if they come back to you they are yours, if they don't they never were."

We speak of love, but really it is the lack of love that we feel far more, the sense of isolation, frustration, conflict with those we love. . . "You always hurt the one you love, the one you'd never hurt at all." We are the meanest of all to those we are closest too. . . parents, kids, partners, brothers and sisters.

"What is love?" I asked my five-year-old this morning, so we could set our parameters to the conversation.

He shrugged, "I don't know."

And nor do I. . . Love is so many intangibles. We try to define and limit it. We try to name it. To say "love is here!" But just when we think we have grasped it, it is gone. Like a butterfly we cannot pin it down without killing it. We know its beauty for a moment, and it is gone. The more we try to grasp it, it eludes us. The more we are open to it, it surrounds us.

What wise children I have. They don't brush their mama's ego when she wants it, nor offer trite platitudes to placate her neediness. They speak their truth, which I discover is my truth too.

How I love them.

Whatever that might mean!

The power of love

And when I feel uncertain,
And when I feel unsure,
I return to the heartbeat,
I return to the womb.

Blessingway Songs: Copperwoman

The first thing our children know is our heartbeat: the rhythm of life. Constant, soothing, lulling, omnipresent, it is the soundtrack to their creation. To be born is to lose the safety of the womb, the gentle thud of togetherness, the mother becomes the other. And for the first time we realize that we are alone in this world. Alone in this sea of noise and pain and cold and heat and confusion.

At times of panic, stress or anguish it is what we crave: the metronome of love, to reset our own.

The power of a parental heartbeat. Perhaps this is the magic of breastfeeding, sling wearing, kangaroo care. Perhaps it is the open chakra of love, radiating into the child. Perhaps it is the primal sense of togetherness, two beings embracing each other, the parental body buffering the storm winds of life, providing the nearest thing to a womb. This is the essence of the mother soul, the Madonna's cloak, this is the balm we can bring to our children and to all who need it. Friends and husbands too often need the healing of the heart, the du-dum, du-dum of pure love.

Nothing has proven the power of the heart more to me than my experience with our three-year-old who is truly terrifying in her strength, her opposition to ideas, and her sheer volume of screaming. Trying to keep myself from reaching overwhelm when dealing with her is one of my deepest challenges. And I don't always manage it.

But if I can stop her reptilian brain system setting off mine (adrenaline production is "infectious"), and hold that calm space for her, and bring her into my body, lying her head on my chest, it has the most incredible hypnotic effect. She settles deep into me, burrowing her head as though she could get right under my skin. Her eyes close, her breathing slows, her head and neck relax, and her body, so often rigid with resistance and aggression, melts into mine. In this state she lets the chiropractor work on her or me wash her hair, the picture of relaxed bliss. And afterwards, her eyes are dreamy and glazed, her voice calm and quiet, her actions gentle and caring. Oh how I need to be able to tap into this more frequently. She has such a maturity for a child her age, such deep loving affection, and the most exquisitely beautiful controlled grace in her movements.

When I see this side of her, when I resist locking horns, butting heads, screaming in total frustration, when I see the beauty of who she is and can be, then I vow to myself to keep trying to work on my own mindfulness, to cut back my own distractions, my delaying tactics, my desire not to engage. She, even more than my other two 'sensitive' children, needs me deeply. And when she and I connect, when her deepest equilibrium is set, and she feels totally safe, totally at peace, not lacking in anything, she is magnificent.

And I have a sneaking suspicion we all are. Truly magnificent. We just need to find the obstacles that stand in our way. We need to balance ourselves and our space, to find our womb, to reconnect with our breath, to listen to the heartbeat of life. And then we might fully love and live as truly magnificent beings.

This was my Dreaming Aloud column from JUNO magazine, Autumn 2011.

competitiveness

One of the hardest aspects of motherhood is the mother war. The battle between opposing views and choices writ large in our parenting. Whatever path we choose, there are others who will often disagree with us, or feel judged or angered by our choices. As much as is humanly possible I avoid the mama wars on my blog and elsewhere.

An end to mama bashing

One of the things I find hardest online is the level of judgment and competitive mama-ing I have witnessed: in forums, on blogs. . . I call it mama-bashing.

I was gobsmacked the first time I witnessed it. It was like a forest fire sweeping round a virtual world. Women around the UK were obviously sat glued to the ensuing battle, their comments flying in thick and fast. Feverish anger, name calling, finger pointing, reputation smearing, and judgments left, right and center.

Mama-bashing. . . the online equivalent to stoning. I felt sick and shaken. And do every time since that I have witnessed it. I have seen it just as often in the natural parenting blogosphere as the mainstream. And it cuts me to the core.

I have never been much good in conflict situations. Mama-bashing is like a playground fight. The sides gather, drawn by a controversial opinion – often genuine, sometimes trollish. If our children were involved in such vicious behavior, we would not find it acceptable.

But instead because smacking is right or wrong, or breastfeeding needs to happen to this age or that. Because sugar/school/doctors are right. . . or wrong (given the forum any of the above can be true. . . or not!) Differences, it seems, are not acceptable.

There is good. . . and bad. And woe betide the person who pokes their head above the wrong parapet to speak their truth, to venture a difference of opinion, to challenge the status quo. Or even to state point blank that they tried this. . . and it did not work. Or circumstances made things this way for them.

Behind the scenes, in private Facebook groups, by text message and in person, there is baiting, bitching, shock, glee, tears, deep hurt. . .

This is my least favorite part of humanity. Especially women folk. And it seems that the anonymity of blogging brings out the worst of it.

So, can I take this opportunity to request an end to mama-bashing? An end to public humiliation, judgment and hurt. An end to stoning the bad woman. To ask that we see the vulnerable mother before the opinion. The woman muddling through under the cloak of apparent certainty. To embrace the whole gamut of peoples' personalities, experiences, situations and cultures. To abstain from supreme judgment, and an acceptance that we are all, deep down, doing the best we can. And those that are not. . . well that is between them and social services, them and their god. Not us on the internet.

In my two years of blogging I have had only one slightly hurtful comment, that I should go and get anti-depressants – though I know it was meant with care. A friend had a similar comment on her blog, which was not voiced so carefully.

And so I am mindful with comments – both mine and others – that the comment usually says more about the commenter than the post. And that what we give out, sets the tone for what we receive back.

Some people find expressing their emotions or deep truths hard, some find expressing themselves in writing hard – don't we all really? Some are communicating in a second or third language, some will be having past hurts or present guilt exercised by your words.

And, as we have discovered in our women's group – the written word is not good for communicating tone – often hurts are no more than misunderstandings: humor or irony not interpreted as they were meant.

And so whilst I respect that others choose to use their experiences with parenting choices to categorically inform others, this is not what I choose for my writing. The only thing I can know with absolute truth is my own experiences, my own ambiguous, ever shifting reality. This I speak as my truth – reclaiming my 'I'.

Because in the end, I do not have certainty. I cannot know that my choices are better than yours. But I can share my journey and how I have come to my choices.

As with all aspects of free speech and controversial opinion, I risk, by speaking my mind, to be judging the judgers.

In the words of Anne Frank: "We all live with the objective of being happy; our lives are all different and yet the same."

This was written for the Carnival of Natural Parenting.

Time poverty and the modern mum

I learnt a new term recently at parenting summit in London: time poverty. The first speaker of the weekend identified it as one of the major factors shaping the modern landscape of parenting and child development.

There was a groan of recognition from the primarily female audience. Yes, we know that all too well, was the unspoken response.

Time poverty: both the lack of time, and, I would add, the perceived lack of time, is endemic in our not-enough culture.

I was reading Brené Brown's most recent book, *Daring Greatly*, and she identifies the pervasiveness of our scarcity culture. When we wake, our first thought is usually that we did not have enough sleep, followed by we don't have enough energy to start the day. Soon followed by not having enough time to be at school or work on time. And so it continues all day: I don't have enough time to do this, enough money to do that. I challenge you to observe yourself tomorrow morning, and then chuckle ruefully at how unconsciously we continually perpetuate this paradigm in our own lives.

Lack of time is my greatest excuse and limitation. When in truth it is more like a lack of willingness to focus, a lack of patience, empathy or an unwillingness to make a decision and stand by it. As well as an abundance of choices. The uncomfortable fact is that our scarcity culture exists in an era of plenty. It is the myth that stands between us and gratitude for all we have. In truth it is a response of overwhelm.

I feel a little in overwhelm after the conference, such a deluge of speakers and messages that I am still digesting. We were encouraged to leave reflections on Post It notes outside the conference room, and one woman observed how she did not know how today's mothers could be time poor, with all our labor-saving devices, and went on to recall her mother doing laundry and baking bread, minding her five children and holding down two jobs, and still she had time to read to them, play and cuddle.

And I felt judged. And frustrated. Because I have time to do that too. And so do you. And we do it. All of us. It's just we do a hell of a lot else as well. And we're not sure how much 'enough' play time, or enough physical demonstration of our love, or time in nature is. And everyone, everywhere is telling us we need to do more of everything. . . literacy skills, and outdoor play, and reading, and singing, and extended breastfeeding and, and, and. . .

And I'm aware that women of a different generation didn't have an ever-growing mass of experts, government and school, giving them more and more (often contradictory) directions. Nor were they faced with the constant looming threat of social services if they were less than perfect. And kids could head off by themselves to wander at large in the fields and roads around their homes.

And I feel this tidal scream of more, more, more, and all I know is that I'm tired, and it's not easy, and whatever I do it never seems enough. And I'm not the only one. Whilst the older generation spoke of wistful hopes for a childhood immersed in love, and away from screens, two of the only three questions (there was not enough time for more!) of the weekend were from mothers of young children. Mothers of intelligence and deep caring who asked with desperate insistence: "As mothers, what can we do, to save childhood?" They spoke for my heart too.

There were no real answers. And this is the crux. We hand our research, our damning views of the future, our blame for laziness and lack of supervision, our anxieties, or incomplete research, and our questions onto the mothers at the coalface. To the world's biggest worriers, the ones with the most invested in these little people of the future. Mothers who are deluged with more information than any mother in history has ever had. And then we baulk when she favors Facebook over choosing from the plethora of contradictory messages that demand she take her kids more firmly in hand, whilst simultaneously giving them more freedom, whilst ensuring they always have adult supervision, whilst they practice independent risk-taking behavior.

No wonder we're tired and overwhelmed. We may not be scrubbing laundry with our bare hands but no mothers in history have been so cerebrally overwhelmed, so vulnerable to constant scrutiny and so alone in their daily task, with such high expectations on their shoulders. And nor have any children in history.

Most of the time it feels like there is not enough of us to be all we are supposed to, and we just need to escape from it all for a moment. Thank flip for Pinterest and Peppa Pig!

Stop with the sunshine!

After speaking to a couple of mother friends over the past few days who feel overwhelmed and despondent, I realize that I'm in danger of turning into one of those annoying mamas who wears hippy skirts, bakes cakes, makes endless craft with their kids and is always happy. . .

Oh, wait a minute, I am that woman.

Hurray! I have made it.

For a while anyway! (Oh ye gods of parenting and clean houses shine your faces upon me forever!)

But let me share a secret with you – I used to read posts by people like me and hate them! Flipping earth mothers! How do they bake their own bread and write a blog and home school and be nice all day?

Well, they are not, I'm sure, and I'm not either.

Two months ago I was bawling my eyes out at women's group because life was shit, I was shit and I hated being a mother and wasn't doing anything, I was barely surviving, let alone baking bread.

So, dear reader, you and I need a little agreement here: just because all is roses in my world today, it doesn't mean everything in your life is not perfect in comparison. So please don't begrudge me the roses.

Oh, comparisons!

We all do it. Yes, even you! Certainly me!

We compare ourselves to other mothers and see ourselves lacking. And go on, admit it, it's not big or pretty, but we sometimes look at other mothers and see them lacking too.

I regularly get the "I don't know how you do it" spiel from other mamas. "I don't know how you bake cakes/ do crafts/ find time to blog/ write. . . " But the reality is, these are things that I value and I love, so I center my life around them. You might not value them as highly as me. You might appreciate them sure, but that doesn't mean you have to do it yourself. You do other stuff.

Maybe you have a beautifully presented house which feels warm and welcoming to visitors. Or you're good at putting outfits together. Or you go running. Or you grow your own vegetables. Or you earn a decent wage. Me, I can do cake. If you're friends with me you'll never be short of delicious homemade cake in your life. But you'll have to put up with mess and missed phone calls.

We each have our own gifts. We know this. . . and still it gets us. Seeing others shine brightly at something can stir up our own unresolved issues.

I read a post on this the other day and committed to writing an honest blow-by-blow account of my life. By 10am I was deeply depressed, stacking up all the little nuggets of tedious misery to share on my blog. So I didn't. And when I let go of that, I had a lovely day! And so I wrote about that instead!

So if you're needing a little reassurance that actually it's completely normal part of mamahood (in our screwed up western world) to be feeling frustrated, isolated and like you're not getting anything done, that actually breastfeeding sucks, you hate being pregnant and actually you didn't get the birth you were promised, please know you are not alone.

I have been there in my own ways – with three kids under five and babies who don't sleep, I have BEEN there – with sore boobs, and wishing I wasn't a mama, wishing long and hard, and shouting at my kids too much and feeling overwhelmed by simply being awake.

I feel you, I know you. And the shit will be on my head again soon enough. But today let me celebrate my sunshine, my glory, my joy.

Super woman and the good enough mum

So I get a lovely email from a fellow blogger: would I do an interview for another blog, on, (drum roll please...) Super Women! What me? (Cue feigned embarrassment)... Why, of course! I know a thing or two about that... Me, Mrs. cake baking, contributing editor, nature table crafting, freelance writer... I AM the essence of Super Woman.

And so I splurge forth my musings on how wonderfully I achieve being me... which I do, actually achieve it, quite wonderfully (though I'd be a bit lame at being you!) And, here's the point: I'm not sure how much help it'd be for anyone, because you'd make a pretty lousy me!

And then the parenting gods struck me down: "Ha! Super Woman, are you? Take that!" – a reprise of the chesty cough and dizzy hot shivers! "And that!": two whingey girls with the same! "And that!": waking half hourly with the baby! "And some icing on your domestic goddess cake?": a really, really messy shit hole of a house and unexpected visitors! "Call yourself Super Woman? Ha, mortal!"

I hastily composed a groveling addendum to my smug interview:

"On reflection, trying to be a Super Woman is precisely my problem! And whilst it's nice to be recognized for what we do and achieve, how we live is far more important. Although most things I do come from my own inner drive, and are often reflective and spiritual, I spend far more time than is healthy in doing, rather than being. This comes at a cost: to my mindfulness, to domestic order and to my own health.

I think the most important thing any person can do is to know themselves and try to find balance amongst the various strands of themselves. And for a woman to know her cycles and her energy levels and work to these rather than against herself. This is absolutely what I try to do. But most often I fail on the balance front – I do too much and then burn out. In our culture this is seen as a good thing. . . but really it's a form of ego driven insanity."

So it was with great interest I received a review copy of *Good Enough is the New Perfect*, a book launched today, based on interviews with 100 working mothers. It is about as far from *Radical Homemakers* as one can get in tone: the mothers featured are all doctors and lawyers and urban corporate types who talk of choosing between thirty nannies and their over-scheduled, over-stressed and high-achieving lives. But still, it had many interesting insights which I identified with.

Their chapter, "The New Mommy Wars", is extremely pertinent, observing that the conflict has moved beyond stay-at-home and working mums, now that the boundaries between these are extremely blurred. Instead women struggle with the multitude of possibilities open to them, and the challenge of choosing the 'right' answers. . . "Who am I? Am I doing this right?"

Each mother's life looks different, because each chooses to put the jigsaw together a little differently based on her own unique priorities, meaning that most are feeling alone in their choices, and unsure if they are 'doing it right'.

The greatest toll of this battle is that we often "forget that what is good enough for someone else, is not good enough for us." Our only guide is a composite of the 'good mom' or 'Super Woman', a cut-and-pasted version of everyone's best bits that we compare ourselves to and find ourselves failing. This is where the idea of the Good Enough mother comes in. . .

The Good Enough mother:

- Knows when to say "I Quit!"

- Knows she doesn't have to be the best at everything

- Stops looking for external approval

- Learns to tune into her own inner voice

- Remains true to her own definitions of success

- Learns to see the 'bigger picture view'

- Knows that individual choices are less important than her overall record.

I wholeheartedly agree.

So off with you, and may you be 'good enough' for you, on your path, in your life, to your kids today.

happy days

These are the happy summer days of future memories. When the days were always sunny and we were free. . .

When we were pirates. . . and painted our own flags.

If not a walk in the park, life was a day on the beach. We count our lucky stars that we live just a mile or so from the shore. Come wind or rain, summer or winter you'll find us there, digging, walking, being. . .

We will remember them as happy days. We will forget the screaming and the hitting and the tantrums and the paint everywhere, the whinging and the throwing food around the room and knocking over drink after drink, and frazzled tempers and feeling overwhelmed

For these truly are the best days of our lives.

Pride

I write very few gloating mama posts. In general one's pride in one's own children does not translate well to others. But every so often, I cannot resist. . .

I see you baby!

Baby Ash is ten-and-a-half months old.

It seems every day we have a new achievement to cheer about in our house. Each day a new example of her finding her own ability to interact with the things of the earth and her fellow humans. Each interaction is an assertion that she is her own person. And each is accompanied by the most wonderful grin of accomplishment.

Some are 'normal' milestones: walking or a first word, though no parent takes these for granted. And some are 'special', like learning to throw a paper airplane after watching her brother and sister do it.

Every milestone for our babies feels like an achievement for us parents too. We have kept them fed and safe so that they might grow. We have weathered the tumultuous first months where life is a blur and the purpose of it all seems far from our grasp. Our helpless baby, whose tiny toes we counted for the first time mere months ago, is growing up. We are all delighting in her burgeoning personhood.

In the past six weeks she has:

Taken her first steps and progressed to running!

Walked out into the garden

Walked around the shops holding my hand

Learnt the dropping game

Discovered that she is most happy with one thing in each hand AND something in her mouth

Discovered how fun it is to race out of the sitting room door and up the stairs as fast as she can *EVERY* time the door is left open

Learnt to lower herself front-ways off the bed without bumping her head

Learnt to support herself in a swing so she doesn't bang her nose

Learnt to clap and bop to music

Drunk from a cup by herself

Learnt to shake her head to great comic effect when she knows she's doing something bold

Held a worm. . . and dropped it

Tried eating everything – favorites include: Lego, stones, dice, chocolate money with the foil on, crayons. . .

Fed herself with a spoon and learnt to spit out food for comic effect

Discovered that the wood burner is hot, and the fireguard is not worth squeezing around

Enjoyed interacting with chickens, piglets and cows

Learnt to throw a paper airplane

Learnt to 'talk' on the phone

Done her first drawing. . .

I am a very proud mama. Can you tell?

Finding our balance

I realized this week that our son is soon to turn six. This summer is a good time for us to focus on physical accomplishments with him: learning to ride a bike on two-wheels, and learning to swim without arm bands. He has had a bike with training wheels for nearly three years.

We bought his sister a balance bike for Christmas, in part to help him to learn. But this week I suggested it. He can be cautious of risk-taking physical stuff – I have no idea where he gets that from!

Since then he has been pestering us intermittently. But things kept coming up. We wanted to give him undivided attention and supervision for this momentous time. This massive milestone.

So my husband took the wheels off after our weekend guests had departed, and then headed inside. I was walking across the lawn to take the tent down. Our boy was on his bike. I held onto him, he popped his feet on the pedals. I pushed a few steps, let go and off he went. To the other side of the lawn. As we say in Ireland, not a bother on him!

No momentous falls or thunder claps. He just could. He already could cycle. And none of us knew.

And it got me to thinking. As these things do. About the times we keep our metaphorical training wheels on longer than necessary. We can cycle. But we play safe. Because we didn't know we could do it alone.

Anger and fierceness

Anger is often left off the list of maternal emotions, as our culture feels more comfortable with the gentle side of motherhood. But we have all been there and know the territory of pure anger that exists in every mother's heart — whether she expresses it or not.

The tiger mother: guardian of boundaries

Tyger, Tyger burning bright, in the fires of the night.

William Blake

When was the last time you roared in anger? Or swiped your claws at someone who threatened something precious to you? Have you managed to contact your tiger mother and hear her roar with awe and pride? Or is she caged and prowling, highly domesticated, de-clawed, defanged and invisible to all?

Since the dawn of human history, tigers have been used as symbols of vibrant strength and fearsome threat. Sculptures and paintings throughout the ages show woman warriors, queens and goddesses accompanied by big cats.

In Hinduism the Tiger Mother, Kali-Ma, is still one of the most beloved of goddesses. She shows a fierce protectiveness over her cubs, a sinewy, animal sexuality, a regal grandeur and great beauty.

> *Her golden black stripes reflect the knowledge she embodies – how to live in the light without avoiding the dark. . . how to reconcile the soft voluptuous sensuality of the golden goddess with the ruthless, uncompromising fierceness of the black Mother who can kill with one swipe of her paw.*

Jalaja Bonheim, *Aphrodite's Daughters*.

My own encounters of the tiger goddess archetype came up around pregnancy and childbirth as I found myself prowling protectively around my house, my lair, and my newborn cub, growling at those who dared infringe too far on my territory.

Even before the birth I found myself sculpting a clay figurine, with a female head and breasts and a tigress's lithe stripy sinewy body.

In birth I evoked this image partly unconsciously as I labored on all fours, feeling totally rooted and strengthened by the ground beneath my hands and knees, my energy circulating through it, swaying my hips and at times throwing my head back and roaring with complete primal power. It was truly one of the most empowering experiences of my life, as the tiger goddess and I became one and pushed our baby out.

I have experienced her many times since, when I have been trying to be a 'good' mother: gentle, patient and forbearing as my children push my buttons more and more, encroaching on my boundaries. I smile and try to distract them, reason with them. I say no still with gentleness, but my hackles beginning to rise, my growl becoming audible in my slightly raised voice. Still they persist, I restrain from swiping physically, but sometimes push them away with a shout. The tiger mother has emerged, the cub warned: you have overstepped.

The tiger goddess is deeply connected to our sexuality, and perhaps this is a crucial part of the birthing equation that we shy clear of in our culture, due to an unwillingness to acknowledge the innate power, sexuality and sensuality of birth.

A mother in the West today is supposed to be ever-loving, ever-giving, and desexualized. This is a denial of our true nature, and a wonderful method of control. We are made to feel guilty when our very real strength rises to the surface. We are taught to swallow our roar and be nice (and trust that we will be protected by others).

Our first step in reconnecting with the Tiger Mother is learning how to say yes and no clearly and mean it, often without negotiation, guilt or explanation,

We have been brought up to smile and be 'nice', when really we want to growl and bare our teeth. The tiger carefully protects her boundaries, both visible and invisible, she will not lash out unprovoked, but stray too close without her permission and prepare to retreat.

We cannot deny this basic nature of ours, and whether we admit it or not, our claws and our growl are there. If not used healthily, they begin to show themselves when we lash out attacking and criticizing others. Or we begin to use our claws on ourselves in self-abusive behaviors such as eating disorders, sexual self-abuse, cutting or substance abuse.

When we refuse to acknowledge and use our rage with clarity and focus to protect justice, innocence and all that we hold most dear, we are not truly rooted in our own power.

When we do not stand in our full power we become victims and martyrs. We begin to lose touch of our other facets: our beauty, our sexuality, our strength.

And when we lose ourselves, all those that love and depend on us lose us too.

The white heat of mama anger

Good mamas are supposed to be nice, gentle, calm, loving, quiet. . . so goes the myth.

Bad mothers are angry, violent. . .

We aspire to be gentle parents. Peaceful parents. Natural parents. So we should know better, do better. . . right?

Wrong!

Some scenes from this week. . . My child keeps pulling out my hair by standing on it repeatedly. The 'baby' presses the delete key on my computer with glee shrieks of delight. The three-year-old kicks her baby sister in the face on purpose, sitting on her, stamping on her, strangling her, and then has a half hour long tantrum because her toast was cut the wrong way. He hates school and doesn't want to put his clothes on and we're already twenty minutes late. She draws on the wall knowing she's not allowed to. He calls his sister "stupid idiot" and "stinky butt", so she wakes up the baby on purpose. She screams: "I'm not going to sleep" for an hour or more every night. Every request I make, every meal I produce is met with screams and whines and complaints. . .

Day after day after day. . .

These days would challenge the combined sainthood of the Dalai Lama, The Pope, Mother Theresa. . . (Are you just a little suspicious that they cultivate such spiritual calm? None have been parents!)

Parenting shows up your yuckiest sides. The sides that, in any other circumstances, you can deny. That until you are up to your eyes in exhaustion, frustration, pain and poo, you do deny. . .

You see, I'm afraid I don't subscribe to the belief that children are born as perfect little angels who should be allowed to express every one of their God-given emotions, whereas all my adult emotions are bad, wrong and to be suppressed. I am supposed to jump with joy when my daughter expresses her anger. But I have to bottle mine. According to these philosophies I have to be kind and gentle and understanding – despite being screamed at, whinged at, pulled and kicked and demanded of on very little sleep.

Sorry, no can do. . . no will do. . . it's not right, normal or fair. . .

I respect I am bigger.

I respect I am stronger.

I respect that they are still little and learning.

I respect that I need to teach them how to handle their emotions and positive ways of dealing with conflict.

I respect that I will not hurt them in uncontrolled anger or with premeditated punishment.

I was smacked as a child and don't agree with it.

And yet. . .

There are times when I have been nice, I have been firm, I have distracted and explained, cajoled and negotiated, shown other ways forward, in gentleness, kindness, giving the benefit of the doubt for tiredness, hunger, age. . . I have taken deep breaths and tried to remove myself from the situation, but the child is beating on the door or hanging onto my leg. . . and actually, you know what. . .

Somewhere, surely there is a place for my expression of physical and vocal frustration, of tit for tat in physical language, look, pinching hurts – demo – so that's why we don't do it. A firm shaking hold – "I feel 'this' cross right now. Do you understand me?" So that they can see that actually I am not a door mat, a slave, a kicking post. I am a human with feelings, just like them.

At this moment very little differentiates me from the mama bear who swats her baby away in frustration – her swat is not meant to damage or injure and nor is mine. It is a warning shot, a physical boundary being drawn. This far and no further, little one, it says. No means no. I said no, I said no again and again, and I mean NO! Now back off. . .

So when my child screams and screams at me and I have exhausted all other options, I scream back. The pure scream from my belly. The scream of frustration. And it feels right. Better. It changes the tone, for us all.

You can keep your pillow pummeling and deep breathing – at this point I need instant physical relief. It is not just my children who have this need. Or this right.

Why is mama anger not OK? And dada anger for that matter? We are scared of it. We are scared of strangers judging us or reporting us to social services. We see stories on the news of hideous child abuse and it puts the fear of our own anger in us. *Could that be me? Could someone think that might be me?* We worry.

The feeling of anger and overwhelm is scary. Parenting books tell us to be calm and patient. These are written by people away from the coalface of parenting, sitting at quiet desks, at professional remove from the simmering cauldron of emotions that real-life parenting brings. Self-help books tell us to express our anger. But not *how* to do this when we are parents.

Anger is a primal emotion – it comes from the reptilian, primitive brain – the part of the brain that does not work with language – so trying to tell our children calmly that we are experiencing anger is both unreal and unrealistic.

I think we must, as parents, show our children what anger really is, how it looks, and how it can burn, though not too deep – the scars of the white heat of anger last a lifetime. I still remember my mother's anger. The physical pain, the terror of this unknown storm, the unpredictability. I do not want to revisit this on my children.

But now I am the mother storm. I dig my fingernails in, my voice rises to a screech, the tears of frustration rain down, my lightning temper flashes... and then the storm abates. We make our peace, the sun breaks through. We are all still here. Survivors. None of us blameless, all a little shaken.

We live to fight another day.

Is the silencing of mama anger a feminist issue?

I have been thinking much over the past few days about mama anger after my post at the weekend. My dear girls are down with chicken pox, part of me is feeling bad about being angry, part of me is relieved that there was a reason for the hellish nature of last week.

Part of me is glad to have shared – I feel an ethical duty not just to show you, my readers, the sunshine, I certainly do not want to hold myself up as someone who has 'got it all figured out' – far from it – the reality of life in my world is not always shiny, not at all. . .

I am glad I touched a chord with many.

I worry that some think I am perhaps a danger to my children or setting a bad example of acted out anger.

I have just discovered a seminal feminist text on mothering, Adrienne Rich's *Of Woman Born: Motherhood as Experience and Institution*. I didn't know it existed, nor did any of my feminist friends, so perhaps you didn't either. One of my major issues with feminism was the lack of acknowledgement of mothering (as I have discussed here before). And so I wanted to share an extended extract from it with you on the topic of mothers' anger:

Opening with a quote she takes from a 19th century manual for mothers, written, yes, by a man:

> "Can a mother expect to govern a child when she cannot govern herself?. . . She must learn to control herself, to subdue her own passions; she must set her children an example of meekness and equanimity. . . Let a mother feel grieved, and manifest her grief when her child does wrong; let her, with calmness and reflection use the discipline

which the case requires; but never let her manifest
irritated feeling, or give utterance to angry expression."

She goes on to detail Marmee's instructions to the hot-tempered Jo in *Little Women*:

"I am angry nearly every day of my life, Jo; but I have
learned not to show it; and I still hope to learn not to feel
it, though it may take me another forty years."

"Mother love," Rich concludes, "is supposed to be continuous, unconditional. Love and anger cannot coexist. Female anger threatens the institution of motherhood."

Seems like not much has changed since she wrote this in the 1970s.

I definitely think when we, when I, scream at my kids, it is more than just screaming at their behavior. It is screaming at the frustration which motherhood brings. The seemingly closed off world and opportunities that the children brought with them, which I didn't fully understand or anticipate. No one can understand the totality of the mother-load until she is up to her eyeballs with no way out. The lack of support, the drudgery which no one can, or will, take from your shoulders. This is the institution of motherhood as our society has built it: isolated, moralized, judged, the mother is expected to be almost everything to her charges. When I scream in anger, I am screaming at the walls of Jericho, willing them to tumble down.

The confessions of a domesticated wild woman

As we head into a New Year, my soul is calling to be free. I am so sick and tired. Literally and metaphorically. Tired, tired, tired of the complications of emotional relationships on every level. Tired of family. This Christmas season has been fraught in just about every family relationship I have, and I am so done with it. All I want is simple: no feelings, no misinterpretations, no demands or requirements made of me. I am fit to run from home and hide in a cabin in the wild woods of Alaska.

May I add as a side note that I am not overdoing it with work, nor with domestic or social commitments. But even the little I am doing is too much. I feel the New Year hovering and with it big new work, new creations to be gestated, others to be delivered. I feel the need to clear and cleanse myself in a way I never have before.

This is not easy as a mama of three little ones. Especially one who wakes throughout the night and does not want to be weaned. And another who demands I do everything for her.

It's all just too full-on in our little world right now – I just need an emotional detox from everything and to step back all requirements that I can. I want to dive into my creative life head first.

And so, with those that understand, I am asking for space. Little kiddies do not, it must be said, understand. So I shall have to do my best. Though in reality I despair of the mother I have become to them. I cannot even justify it many days as 'doing my best'. The truth is that I am here. And that must be enough. I am coming to a rather late conclusion that I am not great long-term mother material. And that does make me feel sad. My creative spirit calls me. I try to keep my heart with my kiddies, not to burn too many bridges. But the call is loud and strong. And I am aware that I am kindling the flames of mother-hate within them, flames that will be fanned by the winds of age and independence.

The voice of the wild calls. I want to be free. The louder it calls, the stronger I feel my weakness as a partner, a mother. My gaping lack of ability. I want to run away, to fly to a far distant land, to be free of my captivity, my drudgery, from this life I have so willingly chosen for myself, from this domestic bliss I have so carefully constructed, piece by piece. It feels like shackles to my soul. It chafes and confines. I long to be free. Just me. Pure, and free. Me and the wind and the moon and the trees, and my trusty pen. Free. How that word sings. I long for freedom. Can taste it like the memory of ice cream eaten on an exotic beach. Everything about my life as a mother is far from free. My day is wound carefully around the needs of others.

I feel like a domesticated wild woman. So often I just want to run. I don't belong here pairing socks and making pancakes, wiping bottoms and lulling fractious children to sleep. I want to be off, wild and free, with no one to answer to, to be nice and polite to, to make a nutritious meal, carefully cut up for. I wish to wake when I want, and sleep when I want. Alone.

I want to write all day, then to sit and watch the fire and eat chocolate and drink too much wine, then walk in the woods by moonlight, before curling up alone in a warm bed with a book that makes my soul soar before going to sleep for a night full of uninterrupted sleep.

Mama's home

So after that last piece, I saw the light. I realized I could ask for what I needed, which was to escape. I asked in love. My husband knew where I was at, knew I wasn't doing a runner on him, and released me with love.

And so I got online, found some wonderful places to retreat – if it wasn't the night before, during the Christmas holidays. . . and so I was left with no final destination.

So I headed for one of my favorite places in the world – West Cork. There is a line that I pass, about ten miles west of Cork city, where the landscape shifts gears, and opens up, and I go ahhhhhhhhh! I feel like I have crossed a kind of time and date line, into a different land, both internally and externally.

So I drove to a beautiful castle overlooking Kinsale bay. It was stormy gusting wind and rain, my tears were appropriate to the day. I sobbed and felt lost. And there, walking past my car, just as I had done on precious times before, were parents walking with their little children. And my heart strings went. That's what I wanted.

You weren't expecting that dear reader, and nor was I. So I drove back past the hotels, past the colorful craft shops and galleries, past the little cafes. I didn't want to eat out, I didn't want a strange bed, and I didn't want to be alone with myself. I wanted home and my children, and my husband, and my bed, and my friends. I missed my baby, I was sad that she would be sad about not breastfeeding. I realized that although I may want to escape from being a mama, I am a mama deep in my body and my soul. Something deep had shifted, unseen, these past few years. I just hadn't had the space to really feel it, to touch it, and so I doubted it was there.

As I was pondering, whether to wimp out and turn around, a friend called to finalize lunch plans, not knowing that I did not know about them, nor that I was over an hour away.

And so I turned my car around and headed for the little fishing village next to ours. And there round a table were some of my dearest friends in the world, a spread of home-cooked food, a baby reaching out to me – "mama, milkie!"

I sat down, late, unannounced and burst into tears. And being true friends, not an eyebrow was raised, not a comment made. My plate was filled – I fed my baby and ate my dinner. And then we talked and laughed and our children played and our menfolk played Scrabble.

Then I had an early night, baby curled in one side of me and my son the other side.

Mama's home!

P.S.

Let it be known that I felt a total wuss chickening out on two precious days alone time, and know that many of my mama readers are yearning for that right now and are probably hurling rocks at me through my computer screen. I just knew that I was getting anxious and needed to be somewhere familiar. So I am taking a six hour creative retreat here today, then a late lunch with other dear friends. And I have special retreat places on my to-do list for later in the year once baba is weaned and I am not feeling anxious.

Growling at our mothers

My five-year-old son is feeling unsettled. Life is not right. Daddy is ill.

He has started rolling his eyes when I talk to him. It makes me feel cross and frustrated. *Respect me*, I think, *I'm your mother*! "I'm your friend," I wheedle, "I'm just trying to help!"

I explain myself more. To which he mutters under his breath and rolls his eyes some more.

I am his mother. I am the font of all his problems. Of course!

This is all a little scary. . . imagine when he is fourteen. . .

I also have two girls. Girls and their mothers. . . oh-oh!

I am 31. I still roll my eyes sometimes when my mother talks. Well, she didn't know this till now (sorry Mummy!) But I do. . . I just do it so she can't see!

And she was 59 yesterday. And she still grumbles at her mum's general failings. Rolling her eyes at her lack of this and that. . . Even though she's been dead for 15 years.

But why?

It means: "Whatever, talk all you want, I'm not listening, I don't care!"

Sometimes it means: "Oh God, stop, stop, you're so embarrassing!"

Sometimes: "Here we go again!"

And others: "Why do I have to tell you. . . why don't you just know?"

Sometimes: "Why do you always have to be right?"

And others: "Why can't you just be perfect?"

I know, from having seen brothers and friends growl at their mothers that this is in fact an act of love. No really! We feel safe enough to communicate our frustration at our mothers that we dare not communicate to others. She is our safe harbor. We trust that she will still love us, even though we growl: something we cannot be sure of with others. She was our soother when we were babies, our everything. We growl because we realize that she is all too human, she has her flaws and failings, she can no longer magic everything better, and sometimes she makes everything worse.

But the thing is, we don't mean it. I may do it. But another part of my brain is listening carefully. Taking it in. And then, when I let my guard down a little, I do what she says. The thing I rejected and yeah-yeahed. It has become a part of me, slipping in under the radar. The thing I once rejected is the thing I now cherish. . . Sorry Mummy! And thank you!

So now I wear colorful tights.

I want pictures of "all of my children together".

I get cross at my children, and then immediately beg their

forgiveness and tell them how much I love them.

I soak dishes so they don't get "welded to the sides".

I go to women's group.

And read many 'odd' books. And talk about sex.

So maybe, just maybe, my voice is going into his head too... With every roll of his eyes he is processing a little bit subconsciously.

Yeah-yeah!

Mindful mama moon time

Over the past four years I have become more attuned to my cycle, or moon time. So much so I've written not one... but two books on the menstrual cycle. I have also become more attuned to the moon's cycles. For the past three years I have been weaving the two together. The impact on my life, and my family's life, has been profound.

I started by focusing on the full moon. By absorbing the high energy during my ovulation and retreating at the dark moon. I had the most common 'white moon' cycle – bleeding on the dark moon, ovulating on the full moon. At ovulation I knew I would be full of energy from both the moon's phase, and my own hormonal balance. As the moon waned, my mood darkened and I would need to retreat, need to take more time to myself, need to remind myself that I wasn't actually angry at the children, but just pre-menstrual and needing more quiet, more head space. In this way I could be more gentle and loving with myself, and therefore with my children, rather than perceiving them as 'the problem'. I knew where I was at with myself. It felt good. So different from the intense, out of control mood-swings of PMS when I got my periods back after our second child.

But then two months ago when my *Moon Time* book was at the printers, and I was feeling full of understanding of my cycle and all women, my cycle flipped to a red moon cycle – bleeding at the full moon, ovulating at the new moon. And what's more, the full moon hid behind winter clouds for two months.

Suddenly I could not look up and know where I was. I felt at sea. Neither rooted in my body wisdom, nor the moon's cycles. I felt wobbly and unsure. My PMS felt more out of control.

I needed an aide de memoire to help me to re-connect to where I was in both cycles. Enter the moon dial – which I now sell on *Dreaming Aloud*, and have sent out to hundreds to women around the world.

This has been my (almost) daily practice since: a simple way of checking in with myself, and with the moon, of grounding myself once more in my own rhythms and those of the heavens.

An interesting addition to this has been noticing how the moon seems to effect the children too. The full moon energizes them, and yet, on a red moon cycle, my energies are low at this time as I am bleeding. This is a challenging energetic dichotomy, but again, one that, now I am mindful of it, becomes easier to manage without blame and anger, but simply by observing.

And so as I write, I am trying to consciously shift my cycle back to the white moon phase, as I feel much more attuned to myself, the moon's energy and my children's energies, when I ovulate at full moon. We are bringing full moon celebration into our family's monthly life together.

The children and I observe the moon together as she waxes, guestimating when she will be full once more. Last month we went down to the beach, drew a labyrinth in the sand and walked it together, before strolling and dancing in the moonlight.

Grief

A mother's grief is incomparable.

Whether for a miscarriage, a still birth, an infant death, an accident, illness or murder it can shake a mother's sense of being to the core. What she needs more than anything is to be loved, to be held, to be mothered herself.

When tragedy strikes, it can often leave us stunned and feeling powerless.

My local community was hit by a tragedy of magnitude beyond comprehension just before Christmas one year. There was a grieving mother in our midst. A whole community rocked with grief.

Once I had moved beyond the shock, the numbness, the surreality of every mothers' worst nightmare, my creative spirit began to unfurl.

I am not a church goer, but I do lead women's circles. And many women were needing to share their feelings of sadness, shock, and deep compassion. And so the Women's Circle of Deep Compassion was born. We baked cakes with rosemary for remembrance. We created beautiful cards of inspiration and love for the mother to treasure. We wrote words of compassion to her. We gathered together and meditated, spoke, prayed, cried and lit candles for all involved. We consciously showered the mourning mother in all the strength and love which we, at that moment, did not need for ourselves.

And I did what comes most naturally to me. I wrote. From the gut. An outpouring of words and tears. An open letter of love and grief that I shared on my blog. Writing it was scary, but a risk that I am glad I took. Not only did it move me on in my own process of grief, but it seemed to touch a chord with so many others too.

The grieving mother soul

Dear mama and all who grieve,

I send you a prayer with every breath. I cannot begin to comprehend your pain, the scale of your loss.

The storm winds of the mother soul howled around this house last night, and every other house in the area. The tears of God raining down upon us as we battened down our hatches and sent continual prayers that you are finding peace and comfort somehow. We are counting and recounting our own blessings with every prayer. Wishing we could transfer them to you.

Words cannot begin to express the sense of deep, deep sadness that every mother and father in our community feels at this moment. We hold our own dear children closely to us, as though we can immunize them and ourselves from suffering and pain through our tiny, repeated act of love, wishing, wishing that this would bring your children back to you.

We wake to a blue sky, the rays of sunshine promising hope. But the mood is dark and somber. The usual school-gate chatter is gone. Even the playground is eerily quiet. We are united in your pain: we are all one.

We want to talk but talking changes nothing. Nor does the news. It is like scratching an itch, it momentarily makes things feel better, and then worse. The facts are not what we want. We seek to find a way through the shock, the senselessness, and the destructive possibilities of the human spirit, the knife-edge of normality which we unknowingly walk along every day that disaster can shatter in an instant. As I feed our chickens and empty our bins, I wish you the soothing tedium of mundanity.

The mother-soul is grieving for one of its own. Know that we are united around you, though you cannot see us or may not know us. We hold the space for you, for you to be as you need, in this moment. We open our Madonna's cloaks, fall into their soft folds, let us hold you and croon you a lullaby to soothe you into sleep and the momentary forgetfulness that it will bring. Let us wail together, let us wash you clean of your pain in our tears, let us feed you and hold you as you cry and scream and rage and then lie silent.

I pray that you might find life after death. Someday, somehow.

With love, deepest love, dear mama and all your family.

Almost

We almost lost our daughter last week.

This is what keeps going through my head as I hold her little, warm body close. Grateful, so grateful for her continuing presence. For the miracle that was. Today and yesterday almost weren't. I am emotionally and physically shaken to my core. As are the whole family. We are now all too aware of the invisible line between normality and tragedy. I am deeply awake to my mother self once more, to the primal biology of the fact that my children are now, and always will be, flesh of my flesh. A fact that can be dulled by the daily drudgery of mothering, the complacency regarding the blessings that my children are to me, to us all.

Last Thursday our youngest, a dainty two-and-a-half-year-old ringletted rascal of a girl fell out of her upstairs bedroom window onto the concrete path below. I got the call at work from a dear friend who was having coffee at our house with my husband. "She's bleeding out of her mouth and nose, but she's crying. I'll come and get you."

I put down the phone and started to run home, hands held in prayer, praying, praying.

The path had a pool of blood. And there in the kitchen, my baby, so small and battered and bloody in her daddy's arms. Crying for me.

I held her. And held her. At home. In the emergency room. All night in the narrow hospital bed. The next day and night. I held her and breathed my prayers. Knowing how close we came to never being able to hold her again. Holding another mother's story in my heart of a daughter who fell from a tree and didn't make it. Showing her little videos of her and her siblings playing on the iPhone knowing that they might have been our last memory. I held her as she slept and slept, knowing that the child who emerged from this tragedy might not be the same one as before. My family have been through the trauma of severe brain injury with my cousin only two years ago. And she was so much smaller. Falling onto concrete. Without a helmet.

They did test after test. Woke her every hour. And beyond possibility there is no sign of internal injury anywhere. No brain damage. No broken bones. No teeth gone. Just a huge black eye and chin. A swollen face. A large infected cut in her mouth and round her teeth. Nowhere that will visibly scar. And incredibly no emotional trauma for her.

I feel sick each time we go down our road. Each cookie cutter house with the same two upstairs windows. The same concrete path. And I know, though it sounds too corny to be true, that the only way she survived that fall is that she was cushioned by angels' wings. And we have been surrounded by them too, in the form of friends and family, in our days of recovery since, as we help heal her body and our parent souls, from the nightmare of almost.

Patience

Patience has never been my strong point. Each year for Christmas and my birthday I ask for the gift of patience. It would make me a much better mother.

I quit!

To whom it may concern,

Please let it be known that I am handing in my notice with direct effect.

I am not sure who would be willing to take on my responsibilities, but am sure that there are plenty more confident/ capable/ qualified/ mad people out there who would be only too delighted to fill this position.

Sure the hours suck, as does the pay, and the employers are irrational and demanding, resorting to regular violent tantrums. But I know that you will find someone else who would have the patience to deal with our three-year-old's meltdowns and demands, who would breastfeed our baby day and night, or just wean her, and would keep the house looking far more respectable. I know many who would kill to be a stay-at-home mama. Right now I feel I could just kill.

I quit. With direct effect.

Sincerely,

Lucy

P.S Can I take the car?

Let's play!

"Let's play!" she says.

"Yes, let's!" I say.

That's the game: "Yes, let's!" It's a game I used to play with my students back in my drama teacher days. Its purpose is to teach actors to accept situations offered them in improvisation situations rather than shutting down and rejecting possibilities. Every idea offered by one player must be accepted with open arms and hearts by the other participants, for example, "Let's pretend we're on the moon". "Yes, let's!"

Only she doesn't know it's a game... or that I'm consciously playing it.

I thought it might be worth a try after yesterday's day of hell on earth with my girl. And after my letter of quittance, another day dawned and I was still in the job. We needed a new approach: a new day called for a fresh start.

I realize that control is a major issue for my daughter (and of course me). In fact it's what most of us want, most of the time, if we're honest with ourselves. She is three. She is a middle child. Her baby sister is quite close in age. She is in need of feeling in control. Of being the leader. And I think this could be contributing to her furies.

So we went to the playground and I played "Yes, let's!" She was in charge. Flitting from swing to slide, to hopscotch to playing pirates. And rather than resist, or saying, "Mama wants to sit down, why don't you play by yourself?" or looking after a baby (who was asleep), I was right there with her.

With every request either with my voice or actions I affirmed her desires, "Yes, let's!" No resistance, resentment, control. I was right there with her, waiting for her lead.

Because it struck me how often children this age hear: *no, not now, leave that, wait, stop that...* What power to give her an hour of yes.

The doula

Today I have been a doula. For a constipated three-year-old.

We tried breathing, and laughing, and distraction, and pushing, and screaming, and squeezing hands, and talking about how mummy pushed babies out of her yoni.

We tried good cop, bad cop. We tried patience and gentleness. We tried insistence. We played hardball and said there was no going to her beloved playschool unless she did one.

It's been three days. . . and counting. . . This child has managed to go eight days before without going. Getting more and more hyper, and cranky, and uncomfortable, and miserable, and sore, and not able to sleep, or eat much.

We have been stuffing her with fruit, and Weetabix and withholding dairy. And getting her to drink lots of water. We have stroked her back and massaged her tummy and read her stories on the toilet and made cooing sounds of sympathy. We have tried singing songs, making jokes, reading books about poo, lying that it won't hurt, threatening that it will hurt if she doesn't do it soon, done huffing puffing birthday candle breaths. . . Oh how like labor this is, I thought. And what a great doula I would make, gently, wisely coaching a woman through.

"Push!" I suggest gently. She ignores me. "Just try, a gentle push," I try again, a little more persuasively, I hope.

"No!"

"A little push, go on!"

"No!"

"Oh, for goodness sakes just push or it's never going to come out!"

How many doulas and midwives resist saying this every day of their working lives? Ah well! I think I'll stick to being a writer!

learning

Learning – whether you choose school-based, or home-based education – is a large part of parenthood, as you navigated the myriad choices and stages, and one that I have given a lot of energy to!

Emotional stew with dumplings on top

My feelings are all of a muddle.

I had been warned by mothers a-plenty that this would happen. But, in the way we all get through life, I had decided that it wouldn't happen to me. That I would be different. I was, after all, exempt from the emotions of other mere mortals.

Yeah right!

So the morning that I have been longing for for almost four years arrives. Ash started playschool today. And now all three kidlets are in school/ playschool five mornings a week.

Am I dancing on the rooftops?

Nope. My mama heart is broken open, sad and lonely. Echoes of silence mock my glee at being alone. I go to a café to be fed and have company.

I am sad. But I know I will be happy.

I feel empty. But know I will be fuller and richer as a result.

I am an emotional stew with dumplings on top!

Change, change, change. That is the only constant in this life. We long for it. . . then suffer through it. And never learn. As stifling as the present moment usually is, the future is often emptier and emptiness opens up space for potential new growth.

But it is only when we have the space that we see how much we are attached to the past that we struggled with before!

On starting school

The time of starting school is here. For those of us who have chosen that path. Today it was our middle child's turn to start playschool. So many friends' children are starting school or playschool this week.

Days of jittery tummies and secret tears for mamas and kiddies. . . and even daddys! Another crucial weaning has arrived. Perhaps we have been counting down the days. But now it's here. And we're not quite so sure. We mentally barter for another day, or week.

How can it have come to this? Our little baby, who we held in our arms a blink ago is here with an oversized rucksack on their backs. Containing a lunchbox made with care, full of their favorites, infused with love, as though each bite of peanut butter sandwich will communicate our love, our best wishes for our precious, brave child venturing out alone in this uncertain world.

There they are dressed and ready. Shiny shoes and a jumper a size too big. The front door echoes as we pull it closed. The queasiness rises. We clutch their hand, smooth their hair, sending up silent prayers.

When we get there, we attend to practical details – the location of pegs, toilets, familiar faces. We hover a little too long. Then move to go.

We steel ourselves. Take a breath. We know they'll love it. We know they'll be fine. We hope. They cling to our skirts, our hands, and our hearts. We settle them again. Take our leave again. Decisive now.

This is the time we wish we were homeschoolers. Then there would be none of this.

Perhaps we peek in the window, or listen at the door. Perhaps there are tears. Theirs or ours.

The morning is a held breath. The minutes like hours. We fill them with distractions – at a café, the mamas gather and share their nervousness. Clutching phones just in case of a distress call. But silence remains. We don't know what to do with ourselves, with this new found time and breathing space. What silence the absence of a child creates.

We return to collect our precious charges. In a few weeks we will be rushing to be on time. Today we are early. Mama and dada racing each other to be the first to see the girl, to clutch her to us, to interrogate her teacher.

She runs out. Noticeably more grown up and sure of herself than the little girl we left there this morning. She knows the shape and size of her own courage. She had fun. We exhale together and share her joy.

And we'll do it all over again tomorrow.

Damn you compulsory education!

We are struggling at the moment.

Really struggling. To send our two children to school. It is compulsory education. For them. For us.

This does not feel good.

For two mornings in a row we have spent nearly two hours cajoling and forcing them into uniforms. Cajoling and forcing them to walk the 100 meters to school. Cajoling and forcing them into their classrooms. And then, after another hour of endlessly prizing the younger one's hands from my neck/ skirt/ arms/ hands, walking away from my child who was screaming for me – even though I had left her one-to-one with the very lovely classroom assistant.

I know she is safe. But she does not.

I know that she will be OK, but she does not.

She looks like a rabbit in the headlights. A trapped tiger. Her need to escape, to be with me, to feel safe is primal. She wet herself.

The teacher wanted me to leave her straight away. She tried to bribe away her tears with stickers. I could sense her desperation as more and more toys and books were pushed her way and questions asked. "Don't feel your feelings" was the lesson she was teaching her. Shut down. Shut up.

She snapped at me for waiting outside the door and "starting her off again." And so I sat with her as the list of rules and controls was explained to the other children. "Don't speak, don't swing, don't wriggle. Don't use the toilet unless you ask. . ."

This is compulsory education.

Twenty six little bodies dressed the same, sat in rows, bribed with stickers to sit still and shut up and color inane shite.

"School is boring!" my seven-year-old son informs me. "I know, my love, I know." This is not my vision of education, I think.

I wish we could run free in the woods, with the river as our guide, the seasons as our teachers. I wish we could paint all day, and get up when we want. I wish I didn't have to force and cajole your precious bodies and spirits to satisfy the powers that be.

But I have learnt too, since becoming a mama – I am not the patient, all-loving, full of energy mama I thought I would be. I get tired, and overwhelmed. I long for peace, to do my work. I am a good one-to-one mama. But there is not one, there are three. Three different characters, different needs – each I want to serve and honor – but the cacophony of competing desires overwhelms me. I begin to sink.

I need to honor you. And I need to honor myself.

We have agonized over school for many years. We have agonized over school for her all year – she is young for her year – but academically and developmentally well above the older kids. She is too young for this year, too old for next. She was getting bored at playschool. Her free pre-school childcare year had been used.

If we "give in", then what do we do? Do we allow them both to homeschool? Do we try to find the money for playschool – which we do not have? Do we teach her that when she tantrums she gets her way?

If we don't then we are complicit in forcing and traumatizing our daughter. We are not honoring her fears and needs. But will homeschooling really be that different? And then all the responsibility for their learning will be on my shoulders.

We are trying a gentler approach, of quarter days, to ease her in. But oh, how I wish there were an easy answer. For her, for him, for us all. One where we all won. One where our days were full of learning, joy and excitement at the world – not fighting and forcing.

Damn you compulsory education!

Summer holidays – sibling revelry

I always look forward to the school summer holidays. Long lazy days. The kids hanging out and doing what kids should do. . .

And then one day into the holidays, I remember. . . What kids do is bicker! A lot. And tease and fight. And bicker some more. And moan that they're bored. And all three demand at once that you have to do *this* for them *now*. And treat you as a short order chef from morning to night. And are around all day creating mess and chaos and dumping their clothes/ toys/ mud pies/ Lego models over every possible surface.

And then I look ahead, nine long weeks in the future and think how the hell are we all going to survive this, let alone enjoy it?

I always swore I wouldn't have kids that bickered. I'm not good at conflict. Being the child of divorce, it sets all my anxieties into over-drive and stress levels through the roof.

And I start to threaten child minders, as I realize what a good idea my working full time would suddenly be.

And we spend every moment we can out of the house to assuage the bickering. . . and instead transport the bickering in the confines of a car with us. . . I realize why homeschooling would have been like the *worst* idea ever. I would have been home in *this* all day, every day.

This is most definitely *not* fun!

And then at some magical point, precisely two weeks into the holidays a transformation occurs. Unbidden. One morning the children wake up, and get up and start playing. Together! And they barely stop all day.

They dress up and play games together, and head out on their bikes, and make mud pies without murders being involved.

In short they realize that they like each other. That they can have more fun together, than killing each other. (Well, they still bicker quite a bit, but it is not their main activity!)

Every year it is the same. And every year I kind of forget. And I don't trust that this shift will happen. Because all I can see and feel is the endless bickering now.

And then I recall that a number of homeschooling families report this transition time too when transitioning from a school-based, to a home-based life. As they adjust to being in multi-age groupings, having less structure to their days, to not being in constant competition and learning to be self-starters rather than organized by others. The sense of freedom is scary at first. There is a lot of energy and negativity that they have to get out of their systems before they find their own rhythm, pattern and modes of interaction again.

So suddenly last week, they started playing. Almost every day they head downstairs in mid-dress-up game – this week alone we've had pirates. . .

And superheroes (I love that Ash is Timmy's mini me – she completely refuses to wear anything girly ever – which I just love. Whereas Meli is a no-trousers girl! Dresses all the way for her, the prettier the better. This girl *knows* about accessorizing!)

Japanese tea parties – replete with fairy sandwiches, and the cherry blossom song and lots of mad bowing.

Dolls' hair dressers and cuddly toy beauty salon.

Lots of Lego with *all three* involved.

And my favorite – Mary, Joseph and the flipping donkey! This is particularly hilarious when you know that we are the only heathens in the village! Baby Jesus seemed to have severe diarrhea in the game, but no worms thankfully and he was expertly breastfed and sling-carried. Joseph was insistent that he was wearing a helmet.

Ah, happy days, with the children who remembered how to play. Bless them.

happy days

The sky was blue.

Not a cloud to be seen.

A boy still home from school with chicken pox – how we are both enjoying these precious homeschooling days. They are just what the doctor ordered.

We made gingerbread robots, stars and planets, investigating the color of Saturn on Google.

We picked elderflowers, identified nettles that sting, and dead nettles that don't.

We crossed the new bridge to the bamboo island and searched for pirates.

And played accordion on the grass (and got bitten by ants).

Ice creams on the beach, drew and walked a labyrinth. . .

Then home to pluck Daddy from the office to swim in the sea. It was like the Costa Del Sol. Water as warm as the bath.

Even baby Ash – who hates ALL water – paddled. . . and almost enjoyed it!

Chips for supper overlooking the sea and fruit salad for pudding upstairs in the bedroom.

Happy days!

highly sensitive

Pregnancy and motherhood can make us all extra sensitive. But about 15-20% of us can be classed as highly sensitive people according to researcher and esteemed author, Elaine Aron.

Most highly sensitive people are very aware of emotional atmospheres and are quite intuitive. They can be hesitant in new situations and are easily overwhelmed in large groups or by too much sensory stimulation.

Highly sensitive children are often labelled shy, fussy or colicky.

They startle easily and hate loud noises. They often have issues with food-intolerance or fussiness, problems sleeping and getting dressed.

Being highly sensitive is not odd or bad in any way. But nor is it changeable. It is a character temperament as real as being born with red hair. Highly sensitive people are just that: highly sensitive to their surroundings. Because of this they can experience sensory overload more frequently than others. This happens when the nervous system becomes stressed and overwhelmed by all the incoming information that they just cannot cope.

The watchful Buddha boy

"The truly creative mind in any field is no more than this:
A human creature born abnormally, inhumanly sensitive.
To him. . .
a touch is a blow,
a sound is a noise,
a misfortune is a tragedy,
a joy is an ecstasy,
a friend is a lover,
a lover is a god,
and failure is death."

Pearl S. Buck

I remember being seven months pregnant and worried that my unborn son might be deaf. I had been to a drumming workshop, and rather than leaping around to the rhythm, as all the books said he should, my normally active baby was deathly still.

Three months later I learnt why. I had a highly sensitive, watchful baby. He did not react or respond to new sounds or sights, but watched, intently, Buddha-like in his serenity, until he was sure he had the measure of them, then smiles and gurgles a plenty.

In his toddler years this little boy commented every time the fridge or boiler clicked on or off, or a plane flew overhead. Whilst the rest of the children in toddler group raced and banged and whooped, he stood aside and observed the madness, noting the tiny wind propeller on the top of the boat's mast outside the hall window.

His modus operandi was always the same: watch, wait and then quietly, gently make his move, carefully, with intent focus. For a while I worried that he was autistic, or something more than just shy or quiet.

I watched him watching the world. Learning his cues, his interests, his fears. There was nothing 'wrong' with him in any way. Though the world seemed intent on telling me so. "How will he manage at school?" a friend asked. "Wait and see," was my reply. "We have to let him unfurl in his own time."

And that's exactly what we did, with gentleness and patience, quietly being with him, helping him learn to challenge himself, but within his limits. Not pushing or forcing, but helping him to ease his way into the world as himself.

The reason we had absolute faith is that he has always been so affectionate, lively and responsive at home. He was quick to walk and learnt to talk 'on time'. He is a real little performer who loves interaction: with people he knows.

But in public we have a different child. In England he is classed as shy, a term I dislike. In Ireland, with a term I have always hated: "strange". Strange means shy with strangers; for babies it means unwilling to be handed from person to person without making a fuss. For a baby to go off with a strangers as happily as with its own mother, that for me is strange. Strange means not smiling at anyone who pokes their face into yours, or their finger into your belly – I wouldn't giggle if a random person did that to me. But then I'm a little "strange" too!

Having read *The Highly Sensitive Person* when I was in university, and found it helpful in explaining many of my 'differences', my mother suggested I have a look at *The Highly Sensitive Child*. According to author Elaine Aron, 15-20% of children are HS, pointers include children who are labelled shy, fussy, faddy, colicky (tick), startle easily (tick), hate loud noises (tick), are hesitant in new situations (tick, tick), have issues with food (tick) amongst many others. The tone of this book is very much aimed at helping you to understand your child, not solve a 'problem.' Aron is careful to stress the many positive characteristics of a sensitive individual.

Our culture is not set up for sensitivity: we are bombarded with noises, smells and visuals from birth; we are constantly overstimulated in our consumer-driven society. Our society does not prize quietness and reflection, but action; not thought, but speech. It demands that our children constantly socialize from the minute that they are born. We are encouraged to stimulate their senses endlessly to raise their IQs from birth, with flashing lights and noisy toys.

I am so happy that we trusted ourselves and learnt about him by watching him and listening to his very real, and slightly different needs, rather than the nay-sayers voices which surrounded us with doubt and worry. I am so grateful for the guidance and wisdom from Aron's book, which I recommend whole-heartedly to other parents. We have the most wonderful, sensitive, thriving boy we could wish for: our precious Buddha boy.

I can't cope – dealing with overwhelm

As a house full of highly sensitive people, overwhelm is something we deal with on a daily basis. I have begun to realize that it is not just my kids' high sensitivities that I need to be aware of in how our days go, but mine, and my husband's, too. I have noticed a pattern, one which leads to meltdowns. . . in all of us.

Jangling nerves, too much noise, too many competing demands, time pressure, hunger, anxiety about being good enough or getting something 'right', tiredness. . . I feel my blood pressure soar, my thoughts racing, my breathing tighten, my voice get shriller, my actions rougher. I need out. Now!

Ten minutes of calm to myself and I can come back to the scene with love, gentleness and a genuine caringness. But up till that point I feel myself floundering, my internal monologue yelling and yelling "*I can't cope, get me out!*"

I say to my kids, "shouting isn't a nice way to deal with people" and then I do it myself. "Treat people gently", I preach, but in these moments I am rough.

I am recognizing in myself, my husband, and my kids the pressure valve, the thermostat which rises to boiling point, the markers that say: *Please stop the overwhelm I can't cope.*

I am recognizing that this is essential for our happy, healthy family co-existence. It is not a sign of weakness or manipulation. It is very real: it is how we function and who we are. Pretending it is not the case, getting angry that it is, blaming others for our feelings or trying to ignore them does not work.

It is at the point of overwhelm our instincts emerge, the reptilian brain literally takes over the show – we lash out, scream, yell. Now is not the time for moralizing, for punishments, for anger. . . now is the time for decompression.

For me I need to physically remove myself to a womb space – my bed, or a small, private dark corner of a room and curl up, preferably with a blanket, close my eyes, breathe and allow the pent up sadness, anger and frustration to emerge – with tears, with the words I wanted to say, with flailing arms and legs. And then to stay there with my breath, until the storm subsides, allowing the dominant negative thoughts to drift away and be replaced with thoughts of love and gratitude for myself and my family.

A way that I help my daughter to deal with her overwhelm, which expresses itself through tropical tantrums, is in my article "Happy Candles" on *Rhythm of the Home.*

My son (aged five) needs to be left totally alone, and *hates* interaction when he feels this way. I often lovingly help him to remove himself to his own space where he can decompress by muttering, shouting, stamping and gradually he starts playing.

We all know that we can request "peace and quiet" when we feel this way. And sometimes the children will be made to have "peace and quiet" as a gentle form of time out, sitting on the bottom step, just to take a breather, get them out of overwhelm and lashing out and give them a chance to decompress.

Two specific situations have happened in recent days where I can see the real importance of being able to hold the space for them as they unwind.

The first is parties. Our son is shy by nature and yet sociable. I understand this contradiction well myself. But large group events like parties are deeply stressful for him, as for many highly sensitives. First there is the anticipation, the worry of whom to interact with and how to break the ice. Then there is the overwhelm of noise, lots of activities, large numbers of people, an unknown physical space, lots of sugary high energy foods. He throws himself body and soul into the party, but when I collect him he begins to come down and totally crashes. His system, at maximum stimulation for so long, is now burnt out – he is tired, dazed, thirsty, feeling sick and often cranky. He is totally spent. Again I totally recognize this from my own experience. This does not mean I always handle it well. I have learnt, from bitter experience that then is not the time to berate him for being ungrateful or being grouchy because he's just had a lovely time. No, then is the time for a quiet story, a gentle DVD, perhaps a bath, some headspace, and then an early bedtime.

The other is times of high stress for physical reasons: doctors' visits, dentists and hair washing time. All three of our children have been nigh on psychotic when having their hair washed (ahem, I have no idea where they get *that* from!) I have noticed that the more mindfully I can be there as I do it, the easier it is for us all. So the first part is to center myself, and to make sure I do not add to the stress by my words or tone of voice. The stressor is discussed calmly in case any real fears need allaying. Then when the time comes I make this clear in a calm voice. I make sure that someone else can take care of the other two children or they are not needing my attention. Then I take them onto my lap (at the doctors) or lying on my chest (at the dentist, chiropractor or in the bath) and make sure they can hear my heart beat, I stroke and talk gently to them until they lie calmly and still. And then whatever the action that needs to happen, does. . . most of the time. And sometimes it doesn't, and we have to try again when we're all calmer and braver.

Right now this mama feels very overwhelmed (I wrote the beginning of this over the weekend after a full night's sleep.) Two very, very broken nights, a very demanding whingey baby wanting to breastfeed constantly day and night, and an aborted attempt to buy new clothes for myself, yes clothes, without holes, in a bright, noisy, overwhelming shopping mall yesterday. We were supposed to be going on a long day trip today, me and the three bickering kidlets. I opted out of that one fast! I am in overwhelm. I need a womb space. I need to curl up. I need quiet. I need out. . . and for one or two moments, whilst posting this blog, my www-womb surrounds me. I have headspace, no one is touching me. In this blog I have discovered another tool for dealing with overwhelm in the midst of family life. I worry that it leads to a lack of being present, the opposite of mindfulness. But for me, I realize, that in order to be present I need to retreat first. In order to be mindful I first have to be able to reconnect with my voice, my self, which so easily gets lost in the maelstrom of family life.

home making

As old fashioned as it sounds, part of motherhood is homemaking. Whether you are a full-time mother or out at work, creating the nest to nurture your babies in is a primitive urge that hits most women in the latter part of their pregnancies. Keeping the domestic chores under control and little mouths fed falls to every mother at some point.

I make no secret of the fact that I am a pretty lame housewife. My head is always somewhere else. And whilst I would love to have a tidy, welcoming haven of a home, the reality is that we're more likely to get that if I make a bit more money from my writing so we can pay a housekeeper to do it. For years I felt like a failure, but now, you know what, I've faced that as reality. Housekeeping is neither a talent nor aspiration of mine. And that doesn't make me a bad mother.

There's no place like home

There really is no place like home. And whilst it was nice to have a change of scene, and the company of good friends, we're glad to be back.

All weekend whilst we were away the girls whinged and wailed and screamed and clung to me for dear life until I thought I might explode. They are coming down with chicken pox, have nasty coughs and were really out of sorts. This is when being home really matters.

What is it with being at home? Is it the simple fact of familiarity, the comfort of having our things around us, or the knowledge that we don't need to be on show? Home holds the space so that we can just get on with being, nothing extra is required of us.

We understand 'home' viscerally. . . even when we're very small. I really got this last year, when we went over to the US, just me and baba, and she, at only three months was out of sorts from the moment we left home, until the moment we got back. They were like this today too. The moment we arrived home, they came back to themselves. They were still ill, but they were home.

Only last week dear hubby and I were discussing if, after a year of living at the Pink House, it felt like 'home'. And you know, it does. Not just because it's ours, after years of living with family and in rented accommodation. Not just because we are able to invest ourselves in the garden, because we're close to family, or in the village of my birth. And certainly not because we've made our 'stamp' on it. Far from it! The interior of the house was lovely when we looked around the house, with the beautiful antique furniture of a single old lady, and very clean and tidy. Now it is filled with the detritus of life with three small kiddies and two messy parents – overflowing with plastic toys, recycling which has been liberated from the bin, three-day-old half eaten biscuits awaiting reclamation by the baba, half-finished craft projects, plants in various stages of aliveness, hundreds of kiddy drawings on paper. . . and walls, a smell that we can't identify, a water tank with a life of its own, lots of scattered cushions. . . on the floor, numerous laundry mountains. . . clean and dirty, and our rather scruffy second-hand furniture.

But you know, it's home. And all the scruffiness is what makes it ours. They are our pictures and books, toys and clothes, our table where so many meals have been shared. It wouldn't grace the cover of any magazine. In my dreams I'd love room for a yoga studio/ teaching room, a writing space, a bedroom for each of the children, a guest bedroom, a larger lawn, an acre of wildflower meadow, a hot tub. . .

It's nothing fancy, and often I apologize for it. But this is home, small but perfectly formed. This is where we get to be us, fully: it is our second skin, like your favorite sock with the hole – tatty but loved. It smells like us, looks like us, it shares our heart, holds our dreams and cradles our togetherness.

The non-domestic goddess shines her sink

Hands up who likes housework?

Certainly not me, as anyone who knows me can attest. I may have acquired the title of domestic goddess for my baking skills, but not my housekeeping ones. If there were a contest for the messiest house in East Cork I would be a strong competitor. In fact I could represent the county in the All Ireland Championships. I despair at the mess in my life and am currently on a serious, sorry. . . fun. . . OK serious/ fun creation of order in my home life, so that our beautiful new home, The Pink House, is not a pit. So that at any moment, a friend/ delivery man/ plumber/ neighbor's child/ Buddha can call in and I am not mortified by our unholy mess.

Householding, especially with so much stuff still in boxes after our move, is a reminder of the stuff we have in our lives, and bodies, that can get clogged up so easily. Healthy houses, like healthy bodies and minds, need to be clear, not aseptic, but not clogged either. The thoughts that circulate round and round and lead to stress headaches and migraines and depression, the fat that clogs our arteries and causes heart attacks, the back log of faeces that causes constipation. These are internal versions of the piles of shit that we have in our houses that we don't deal with.

I am not a tidy person by nature – I read eight books at a go and have multiple craft and writing projects 'in progress' at any one time – but I do feel good when my surroundings are clear. I work best when energy can circulate easily, and I'm not looking at clutter on every surface. I know that I am happier when our house is tidy. I am more creative. And more sociable. So it's all good. Except someone has to do it!

I have some serious obstacles to my tidiness aspirations: 1) a messy me, 2) a messy husband 3), 4) and 5) messy children 6) the fact that I infinitely prefer spending any downtime, even non-downtime, writing, crafting, cooking, reading, watching *Come Dine with Me. . .* So what to do?

I have heard from a few sources of a wonderful woman called Fly Lady so I looked her up, and took a few tips on board.

So now I shine my sink every night. And sometimes I managed to cleanse, tone and moisturize my face too! I have identified the clutter attracting 'hot spots' in each room. And deal with them every day.

I also have my season's table/ nature corner in the hall, so that it is the first thing you see as you enter – a little altar celebrating nature's bounty and our creativity with fairies, gnomes and little creatures to animate the scene. This ensures a clutter-free, well-tended, inspiring sight when I walk in the door.

I am trying to find places for everything to live. And persuade children that a hook is indeed a good home for a coat, rather than the middle of the floor.

We are setting up storage solutions everywhere. Passing on what we no longer need. And being mindful of the following motto when we acquire new things: "Have nothing in your life that is not beautiful or useful." Though I have another shopping basket stacking up on Amazon. But you can never have enough books!

Speaking of books, I have always loved the idea – in my favorite Iris Murdoch book, *The Good Apprentice* – of carrying spaces: places in the house which you put stuff that needs to go, say, upstairs, and then when someone passes there, they continue it on its journey.

In this way, may our house, and all its inhabitants be happy, healthy, calm, ordered, and know where to find their shoes/ socks/ phone/lunchbox/glasses/Cinderella book in the morning. Here's hoping!

Radical Homemakers: of housewives and feminists

Is this it? I wrote in my journal a few weeks back, after weeks of being housebound with a sick family and icy roads. Endless cooking, cleaning, tidying, more tidying and yet more tidying with little other distraction had taken their toll. *I'm a $@*#£! housewife!*

I have nothing against housewives: I just never intended to be one. For good reason: I am a *terrible* housewife. I cultivate cobwebs and laundry mountains in my home with as great success as the carrots and parsley I grow in my garden. I try to breathe mindfully whilst I do 'my duties', rather than fuming against my family, my husband and biology. I would not class my domestic skills (except cooking) anywhere in my top twenty of 'things I'm good at'. They don't come naturally. I don't enjoy them. In fact, often I feel like I would rather gnaw off my own arm than empty the dishwasher or tidy the toys for the umpteenth time today.

A brief history of housewives

Housewives, argues Shannon Hayes in *Radical Homemakers*, are an aberration of our consumer culture. According to her "the household did not become the 'woman's sphere' until the industrial revolution."

Housewife and husband were related terms. Husband meaning bonded to his own house, rather than to a lord. In the past men and women shared a home based life with a division of labor according to tradition and skills passed down over generations. Men doing leather work, chopping wood, butchering animals, threshing, fire making, woodworking. Women would play their part childrearing, cooking, preserving, tending kitchen gardens, healing. Domestic work was valued, requiring skill, creativity and ingenuity, and was satisfying.

But economics changed this, first drawing men, then women out of the home. No longer would home be a place of family, food production, education, work and leisure – instead all of these functions were externalized, and bought, requiring money, and thus further work outside the home, and round the circle goes.

One of the key texts to which Hayes' *Radical Homemakers* refers in her historical analysis of the development of domestic life in America is Betty Friedan's seminal text, *The Feminine Mystique* (1963).

> *Friedan details 'housewife syndrome' thus: 'American*
> *girls grew up fantasizing about finding husbands, buying*
> *their dream homes and dream appliances, popping out*
> *babies and living happily-ever-after.' In truth, pointed out*
> *Freidan, happily-ever-after never came.*

She documented the loss of potential, the depression, boredom and bewilderment of post-war American housewives, and spoke of 'the problem that has no name'. Her words hit the American psyche deep, helping to spark the second wave of feminism in the 70s, and sending women out to work, and away from their homes, in droves.

> *Before long, the second family income was no longer*
> *an option. In the minds of many it was a necessity.*
> *Homemaking, like eating organic foods, seemed a luxury*
> *to be enjoyed only by those wives whose husbands garnered*
> *substantial earnings. . . At the other extreme homemaking*
> *was seen as the realm of the ultra-subjugated, where*
> *women accepted the role of servants to their husbands*
> *and children. . .*

I remember clearly reading *The Feminine Mystique* at university, as part of my self-appointed women's studies. I may have been studying a degree, but also found myself doing far more than my fair share of housework in my apartment with my then-boyfriend, now-husband. My head may have been full of feminist furor, but my heart was heavy with the knowledge that my ovarian ownership meant that our culture would expect the domestic sphere to be mine, especially if I were to 'opt' (for me it is not a choice, but a pre-requisite) to 'stay home' (it's *work* people, just not paid!) with my children for their early years.

I had put so much of my time and being into attaining top academic achievements through to graduate level, I was not prepared to give up my creativity or life of the mind to keep house. Nor was I prepared to sacrifice my deep soul need for a homemade home and loved family and kitchen garden for a glittering career and loadsa money.

This was deeply problematic for me, because on the one hand I have the anti-tidy gene and on the other I am deeply attracted to self-sufficiency. I have always aspired to a home based life: cooking, preserving, growing my own veg and sewing simple bits for my home.

It was reading *Radical Homemakers* that finally balanced these two aspects for me. When the reader is ready, the book comes along! Hayes' book gave me the confidence boost I needed: I am not a struggling, failed housewife. I am just an over-whelmed Radical Homemaker with three very young children.

Enter our life, one that many of our friends share too, which I had always struggled to pin down. Yes, on the census form we are "housewives" but in reality we, and our partners with 'job titles' are so much more. The lives we lead so much richer and diverse than any existing definition. Before reading *Radical Homemakers* I had no word for what we were, no framework for what we were trying to achieve. It felt so slippery, that when I wasn't 'achieving' it and feeling miserable I found it so difficult to articulate why. This book has given me terminology.

Firstly the term homemaker, which for me had always been a slightly awkward Americanism, suddenly made more sense. The distinction between a housewife and homemaker is an important one. Whilst Americans have moved over to the term homemaker in common parlance, in the UK and Ireland we have tended to stick with housewife. Housewife connotes both a woman, in her role as wife, therefore in relation to her husband, not her own person. And also wedded to her house, an object, a possession of status. Whereas homemaker is firstly gender non-specific and secondly speaks not merely of an economic asset, but a place of primal belonging: a home.

So what is a radical homemaker? According to Hayes it is:

Someone who wasn't ruled by our consumer culture, who embodied a strong ecological ethic, who held genuine power in the household, who was living a full, creative, challenging and socially contributory life...

These families did not see their homes as a refuge from the world. Rather each home was the center for social change, the starting point from which a better life would ripple out for everyone.

Yup, that's us!

How about you? Will you join us?

Spring clearing

Every so often I feel the clutter in our house build up to screaming point... or suffocation levels.

When I have been preoccupied with big creative projects, or sick, both of which I seem to spend a lot of time doing, I don't have the energy or headspace to do anything other than get meals in front of people, keep the mountain of dishes from toppling and burying us alive, and making sure that homework gets done most nights. But the clutter builds and grows.

Our girl turned six yesterday. The kids have just switched rooms, which required a swap of belongings, and trying to configure a way for our eldest and youngest to share the biggest bedroom in a way that works for them both.

Our room needs reorganizing too. The first thing that needed to happen was to clear off my dressing table, which also acts as a minor altar space.

Ahhh, breathing space... what had seemed to impenetrable and overwhelming, was sorted and cleared in a matter of minutes.

And then I moved on, patch by patch, through my bedroom. I sorted my new bookshelf, which I hadn't even been able to reach, and re-organized it shifting my books I live by to it, and bringing others up from downstairs which I previously felt vulnerable about visitors, especially my mother-in-law seeing. . . you know the *Vagina Monologues* sorta thing! And another little altar went on top.

And then onto the kids room. . . Seven bin bags of clothes and three large boxes of books for charity shop. Five bags of rubbish, three of recycling. . . I feel really proud of myself. We now have spaces that reflect our needs and passions. . . we are at home here. . . and no longer camping or living out of boxes.

There is space to think. . . and breathe. . . for the light to shine in. It is clear. There is space for spring magic.

Cooking with love

Buddhists say that the way we do things influences the results. If we cook with love, we transmit that love into the food, and into those who eat the food. If we cook in mindful awareness, then we can quietly observe with our senses rather than forgetting the cookies in the oven, or adding too much salt because we are distracted. When we are there in the moment, we can be responsive and creative. When we are aware, we can consciously season our food with love.

The proof of the pudding, as they say, is in the eating. Or in yesterday's case, not pudding but hummus. I was cross yesterday: tired, over-stretched and trying to do too much with too few resources. And so it was with huge anger and resentment I made my little boy some hummus. My temper was sour, so I added too much lemon. Then I tried a quick fix by chucking in a pinch of sugar. What I should have done was to calmly detach myself from the situation, taken a few breaths and come back to preparing food with love, rather than banging and slamming and making inedible food. My little girl took one mouthful and spat it out in disgust!

I remember fondly the part of Laura Esquivel's beautiful book *Like Water for Chocolate* when Tita cooks her passionate emotions into the food – once serving up a rose petal sauce which made everyone passionately amorous, and another day a dish which made the assembled party distraught with misery, as though the tears she cried into the pot as she stirred it were infectious.

I am thinking a lot about food at the moment: cooking and the production of the basic foodstuffs.

If we accept that the way in which food is produced has an impact on us, not only our physical health but our emotional and psychological well-being, then it is vital that we support food production practices which support people, the environment and the earth. It is crucial that we cook and eat at home to consciously produce well-being for our families. Perhaps that means cooking more, and ensuring you eat together at least once a day. Or perhaps (note to self) it means cooking a little less, having fewer expectations, a little less greed, but doing what we do with total devotion to ourselves, our families and giving thanks for the food, the animals that gave their lives, the farmers who grew the vegetables. Cherishing our food as we cherish ourselves.

Thich Nhat Hanh, the living Buddhist philosopher, asks us to contemplate an orange. What do you see? Not just an orange, but the rain which fell to make it grow, the earth, the tree, the woman who picked it, the man who packed it, the lorry and the roads it passed along, the wife who fed the lorry driver, the work we did to make the money to buy the orange, the factory where the bag was made to hold the oranges together, the oil that the bag was made from, the depths of the Earth from whence that came. In everything he asks us to contemplate the deep interconnectedness of all things.

There is nothing simple or inevitable about the food that lands on our plates. It is a combination of love, hard work, miracles of nature and good fortune which allow us to have such an abundance of food when so many others do not. At this time of feasting, let us feast with awareness and gratitude.

Christmas is coming and mama's getting panicked

Having got hyper-excited about Christmas back in September, and decorated the house on 1st December to occupy sick kiddies, we are now less than two weeks to Christmas, only six days till my mum arrives. I need to get motoring.

I have lists to write you see, and lots of them – shopping lists, cooking lists, Christmas card lists, gift-wrapping lists, meal lists, lists of lists. . . and soon there'll be thank you letter lists too!

Reading Delia's Smith's *Christmas* book in bed this morning, post-it note bookmarks to hand, she gently says "to avoid panicking, you should get planning and write lists in mid-October."

OCTOBER!

It's now mid-December. I have no lists. I am panicking. So no more creative writing for this mama, (boo hoo!) instead I will be writing lists.

And bleeping Christmas cards, addressing them (by memory as I've lost my address book, grrr!) Though I do have everyone's presents bought. Hurray!

The house smelt of Christmas last night, as I simmered a cranberry mincemeat on the stove – wafts of orange, cinnamon, port and cranberries greeted my husband as he came in from the cold. Heaven!

But this is only one cooking achievement from a very long (yet to be written) list of Christmas delights that I want to make.

I don't feel like having a half-hearted Christmas, but fear that exhaustion will get the better of me. I want to be that domestic goddess whose home looks like something out of *Martha Stewart* – all elaborate wreathes and garlands, bronzed turkeys and matching napkins.

But the kiddies won't let that happen. So instead we'll do it our way. It will be homemade. . . and look homemade.

Today we made paper chains, before the breakfast plates were even cleared. And now Number One child is hassling me to make more of them, and star stained glass windows. . . And of course the dreaded (by me) gingerbread house which will look nothing like those masterpieces you see on Pinterest, but rather a tumbledown shack that will be stripped of its sweets whilst the toffee is still hot!

We have a festive women's group here tomorrow, where we'll be making embroidered felt decorations and drinking mulled apple juice. Sans kids. A moment of communal aspirational domestic goddestry!

But now back to lists: a chocolate yule log, jeweled panforte, ruby cranberry sauce, spiced nuts, ginger glazed ham, steaming mulled port, cider with buttered apples, cranberry and white chocolate cookies, chocolate dipped orange peel, choc cherry cupcakes. . .

Christmas is coming and mama will be gettin' fat!

A mothering badge of honor for a day well done

We live in a culture where what is valued is rewarded with money, medals, certificates, public acclaim. But for those of us that parent at home, all those badges are notably absent.

Oftentimes I give myself a hard time. For not being perfect. For being crabby, impatient, sarcastic, frustrated, even a little shouty. For serving my family a ready meal. For having a messy, messy house. For having the day before yesterday's washing up still stacked by the sink. For having a laundry mountain the size of Kilimanjaro.

Today, however, was different I give myself top marks. Today I earned my mama badge of honor for a good day's work. Issued by myself. And so I share with you my day: the highs and lows of being a stay at home mama, the drudgery and simple joys of this, my path, which may be yours too. . .

I woke multiple times in the night to breastfeed my baby. . . and wasn't resentful.

I was woken just after dawn by a tumbling of children crawling all over me and scratching my face. . . and I didn't shout.

I cooked porridge that wasn't eaten.

Made a packed lunch that was.

Brushed my hair (it doesn't happen every day!) and put on clean tights (ditto!)

I MADE MY BED!!!!

Unloaded the dishwasher. I hate washing up and dishwashers, but I didn't think bad thoughts whilst I did it today, so double brownie points!

Got myself and two girls dressed without a tantrum (I'm a terror for tantruming when I get dressed – just ask my mother!)

Got to playgroup. EARLY. And it wasn't my turn. And so set up.

Sold five books and a copy of *JUNO*.

Cooked a rather yummy mushroom soup and hummus for friends who came to lunch.

Managed to light the wood burner – that alone deserve a gold medal.

Baked and iced gingerbread men *with* my children.

Tidied house and loaded dishwasher and did a load of washing – blah blah. . .

Did much *JUNO* administrative correspondence and bagged myself a review copy of a book I've been wanting for ages – score!

And checked my blog stats once or twice, and saw that 50 people read my last blog post – thank you people!

Cooked supper. . . and pudding.

Didn't shout at my two year-old once. . . even though she asked to stir the custard in the jug a million times in a whingey voice. . . or when she wouldn't put on a top and it's freezing today. . . or when she spilt her custard. . . or when she wanted a red straw and we didn't have one. . . or. . . you get the picture.

Helped my baby practice her walking.

Averted a very messy World War Three when two children were fighting over wanting to poo in the same toilet.

Wiped a lotta botties.

Helped put the older two hyper kids to bed before dealing with baby.

Oh sugar, just realized I forgot to do homework with my son – oops! That's one to add to tomorrow morning's to-do list.

And was nice to my husband *all* day – that certainly doesn't happen every day of the week (sorry, love!)

And gave myself a pat on the back for an under-appreciated and unpaid job well done, and rewarded myself with a hot bath, watching a little cookery porn, sorry, Nigella Lawson, on the telly, and took to bed early. . . to write a book review on the fact that the end of the world is nigh – ah well!

And I'll do it all over again tomorrow.

And so, dearest mama, will you. Give yourself a gold star too.

And if it wasn't a gold-star day, then know that tomorrow is a whole other day, so don't go beating yourself up. You get LOTS of practice at this mothering/ domesticity lark.

playful

Where children are involved there will always be humor. They will make you laugh at them – and yourself – which adds some wonderful light relief.

I am an idiot

So thinks my two-year-old. Her evidence?

I do not know how to cut toast. There are a range of possible options: life jackets, circles, birds and 'big ones'. All with a sub-set of variations of crust/ no crust combinations. I cannot be trusted to read her mind as to which of these combinations is required right now.

Ditto spoons. Is it the pink one? The baby one (also pink)? Timmy's one (a different shade of pink again)? Or a 'people's' one (adult spoon)?

I cannot, under any circumstances be trusted to put on socks. This is the domain of Dada.

Ditto pulling up trousers. I pull them up too high. Apparently. Ditto pulling down trousers to pee. I pull them too low!

So people, there you have it. You are wrong, Cambridge University were wrong. . . I am neither wise nor clever. No, I am a banana. A potato. A slug. An idiot!

Jesus in a space ship the zany world of a five-year-old boy

My son started at the local school this September. 95% of Irish schools are Catholic. Irish schools have a required 30 minutes daily religious instruction.

We, however, are not religious. Not in any shape or form.

But we want our children to be integrated into their community.

Which means sending them to the local village school.

How, we wonder, will this work?

And so today, a conversation started in our house.

"Who lives there?" I asked "Jesus?" I can't remember exactly where this place was we were talking about, but I was being playful.

"No, mum, Jesus lives in Heaven" *Duurgh!* said the tone of his voice, this is a serious topic.

OK, methinks, let's see what he's been taught. And so I lead a serious line of questioning.

"Who else lives in Heaven?"

"God, the Father and Holy Mary!"

Cue sharp intake of non-believer parental breath.

"And will you go?"

"No," he replies, quite clear on that, "No children there. We're here on Earth."

"Where is Heaven?"

"Up there in the stars," he says pointing up.

"So how did Jesus get there?"

A momentary pause for thought... "In a spaceship!"

The conversation continues with conjectures about Jesus talking to aliens and the Holy Mother and God the Father having spaceship races.

Oh the joy of five-year-old logic.

God bless the aliens!

The Game of Life

Our family's favorite game at the moment is The Game of Life. That '80s classic board game, which I, in turn, loved as a child.

It's a great allegory for this game we call life. We take it all so seriously. But it is just a game in the end. We spin the spinner, sometimes we race forwards, otherwise creep slowly, sometimes we win, sometimes we lose. Marriage, kids, money, careers come our way, or are taken away.

I play the game differently, as an adult, than I did as a child. A little more philosophically. But still. . . I don't want to lose. None of us do.

We play it in quite a different way with our children (eight, six and four) in 2014 than I did as a child. A way I could have never conceived of in the '80s.

Instead of automatically being assigned a pink or blue peg according to the anatomy they were born with, our kids choose their color. . . This might sound trivial, but we try to allow our children to find their own way to express their identities, and felt sense of self, independent of social gender constructs. All the while discussing the issue of social perception and judgment with them. Our boy at the age of seven chose to grow his hair long. It is half way down his back now, and almost daily he is mistaken for a girl. He is philosophical about it. He has his own internal reasons for wanting his hair long and is not going to be shifted by the discomfort of others. His favorite colors are orange and blue. . . but he says he likes pink too.

Our youngest girl has often been mistaken for a boy. She lives in jeans and corduroy trousers, her hair is the shortest of all the kids, and she loves dinosaurs, Bob the Builder and Thomas the Tank Engine. Her favorite colors are blue and green. But she is very clear she is not a tom boy. This is just what she likes.

Our middle girl has a 'dress only' policy. The pinker and frillier the better. It's Barbie dolls and Disney Princesses all the way for her. She also loves art with a passion I recognize. And digging mines in the garden. Her pretty dresses are usually covered in paint and mud, which is, in my humble opinion, exactly the way it should be.

So once you've picked your identity... and the color of your car... (all the essentials of life!) you're on the start line.

So first you have to choose – just like in real life – 25K of debt... but a bigger choice of careers open to you... or risking a crappy paid starting job... but start earning straight away. My husband and I were 'University all the way' people, in life... and the game... but now we see the big benefits to diving straight into life.

It's still a little old fashioned so marriage ALWAYS comes before kids... but then... bring the kids on! Or perhaps not. Whether you have them, or how many is up to the wheel of fate... as we know from our own experience.

So marriage... in the 2014 version, we choose the gender of our partners. As a child I always got myself a husband when I reached the enforced marriage bit. I'm not sure I even knew what 'gay' was aged seven. But our kids do... they know and accept gay partnerships as a normal form of human coupling. Gay weddings are *de rigeur* in our Game of Life.

Then it's regular pay days. Big expenses that wallop you when you least expect them...

Then, just as everything feels like it's going smoothly...

Know the feeling?

And right at this point you start acquiring Status Symbols. The more the better.

I'm embarrassed to admit we have yet to get our own oil well yet in real life – but obviously we have a fine collection of antiques, racehorses and Rolls Royces, not to mention the beach villa and private jet. . . so we can still be friends, right?

Playing The Game with my kids, I see mapped out ahead of them this Western capitalist map, of all the twists and turns of a Western capitalist life, and the passive role that they are expected to play – drive your car, do what you're told, when you're told. All so astutely put down in the '80s heyday of our culture. . . What bothers me is it's all about the money, money, money, and blind fate, and conventional careers.

We all love it, sure, but I'm wondering an alternative version: one which reflects more truly who we are as a family. A transition times version of The Game of Life. Squares might include:

- Start a commune, add an extra person to your coconut oil powered tuk-tuk

- Conscious Uncoupling – pay 50,000 for mediation and therapy

- Start growing your own veg – receive 2,000

- Leave your kids unvaccinated – pay 5,000 fine

- Plant a forest, have an extra go

- Start homeschooling – take a new career card

- Your book appears on *Oprah*, receive 100,000

- Karma bites your ass, miss a go

- Spend 10,000 on a Vision Quest

- Your windfarm is successful – receive 150,000

- Cannabis is legalised – spend 2,000 on a party to celebrate

- Give away a status symbol and have another go

- Swap places with someone else – learn compassion!

I might even put stickers over some of the more 'traditional' squares!

A mother's prayer

All mothers,

Who art down the road, in the house next door, all around the world,

Hallowed be thy names.

Thy time will come, thy work will be done.

You give this day the daily bread – endless sandwiches (with crusts off, and cut the right way), wraps and pittas, with hummus or ham, jam or peanut butter, with butter or without, that will be left half-eaten.

Forgive us our shouting and lack of patience.

As we forgive those grubby fingered little sods who drew on the walls with our lipstick, sat on their sister, spat out their dinner and said mean things to their brother, and decided he'd prefer another mama.

And lead us not into temptation – three slices of cake is enough for a mama, and the grass is not always greener despite what you might think.

But deliver us from repeating cycles of abuse, hurt and destruction upon our precious charges.

For theirs **is the** future,

The power and the glory are not apparent right now.

Forever, and ever, and ever they seem to take to go to sleep, and it all seems a blur,

But one day we will see the results of this daily drudge and give thanks for our part in this miracle.

Ah men, don't know how good they've got it. . . or what they're missing out on!

About the author

Lucy H. Pearce is a third generation Creative Rainbow Mama trying to honor her diverse creative urges (writing, painting, teaching, community-organising, publishing, baking, editing, world-changing...) and her need to be a hands-on, engaged mama to her three home-birthed children, now aged 9, 6 and 4.

They live in a little pink house with white shutters, in the village of her birth on the south coast of County Cork, Ireland. Her family sit on the white picket fence which divides the mainstream world from that of the hippies – and they like the view!

She is the author of five life-changing non-fiction books for women including the Amazon bestsellers *Burning Woman*, *Moon Time: harness the ever-changing energy of your menstrual cycle*, *Reaching for the Moon: a girl's guide to her cycles*, *Full Circle Health: integrated health charting for women* and *The Rainbow Way: cultivating creativity in the midst of motherhood*.

Lucy is an award-winning graduate in the History of Ideas. Former contributing editor at *JUNO*, she wrote her popular column, Dreaming Aloud, for the magazine for almost five years. Her writing has appeared in major book anthologies (Tiny Buddha, BlogHer, Wild Sister), newspapers and magazines around the world. She is much in demand as an inspirational speaker in the field of women's creativity and the menstrual cycle.

Together with her husband, she runs an editorial services business, Lucent Word, and Womancraft Publishing, which publishes life-changing, paradigm-shifting books by women, for women. They are champions of new technology, building strong collaborative, creative partnerships and fair profit sharing.

Her blog Dreaming Aloud.net, a finalist in the 2014 Irish Blog Awards, started in 2010. There she muses on creativity, motherhood, mindfulness and taboo busting.

Her website, The Happy Womb.com is a much-loved repository of empowering resources for women.

Lucy has also become known for her vibrant visual art and her work has been commissioned for magazines, book covers and family portraits. lucy-h-pearce.artistwebsites.com

You can contact her by email at: lucy@thehappywomb.com

You can find out more about Lucy and her work on her website, dreamingaloud.net, along with her art, e-courses, online shop and event schedule.

Also from Womancraft Publishing

Moon Dreams Diary by Starr Meneely

Taking the form of a diary, *Moon Dreams* is a simple yet powerful tool for charting your cycle and the moon and a gentle, guided introduction to this practice.

A beautiful first moon gift for a special girl in your life who is coming of age, for a mother starting her cycles again after birth, for women charting their fertility, or any woman who has been searching for a supported way to chart her cycle.

Moon Dreams nurtures mindfulness, reflectiveness and awareness of our body, feelings, menstrual cycle, and the cycle of the moon.

- 52-week diary
- Space to doodle
- Beautiful illustrations to colour
- Information on charting your cycle
- Learn about the moon's phases and how they affect you
- Quotations to inspire and uplift
- Private space to reflect

Moon Dreams is exactly what womanhood needs right now. This journal will set young women on a path of mindfulness, self-love and connection with the wild, beautiful, natural world around them. It has the potential to be life changing; it reclaims our menstrual cycle as a sacred, powerful experience, rather than the revolting weakness that modern society seems to view it as. Every woman needs to get her hands on a Moon Dreams journal!

Lucy AitkenRead, *Lulastic and the Hippyshake*

Liberating Motherhood by Vanessa Olorenshaw

If it is true that there have been waves of feminism, then mothers' rights are the flotsam left behind on the ocean surface of patriarchy. For all the talk of women's liberation, when it is predicated on liberation from motherhood, it is no liberation at all. Under twenty-first century capitalism, the bonds of motherhood are being replaced with binds to the market within wage slavery and ruthless individualism. Mothers are in bondage – and not in a 50 Shades way.

Vanessa Olorenshaw is clear: when mothering is on our terms, it can be liberating. The time has come for a radical, bold and creative approach to the question of mothers, children and care.

Liberating Motherhood discusses our bodies, our minds, our labour and our hearts, exploring issues from birth and breastfeeding to mental health, economics, politics, basic incomes and love and in doing so, broaches a conversation we've been avoiding for years: how do we value motherhood?

Listen up – Mummy's got something to say!

Highly acclaimed by leading parenting authors, academics and activists, with a foreword from Naomi Stadlen, founder of *Mothers Talking* and author of *What Mothers Do*, and *How Mothers Love*.

Lucid and riveting, this book sweeps you along to a realization that we are at a turning point in history. That even feminism hasn't asked big enough questions. Our humanity depends on re-elevating the nurture of young lives to our most primary purpose. Olorenshaw speaks for a generation of young women who are refusing to have their hearts numbed and their yearnings suffocated for corporate greed and a feedlot existence. This is The Female Eunuch of the 21st century.

Steve Biddulph, bestselling author of *Raising Boys*, Raising Girls, and *The Secret of Happy Children*

Burning Woman by Lucy H. Pearce

The long-awaited new title from Amazon bestselling author Lucy H. Pearce. *Burning Woman* is a breath-taking and controversial woman's journey through history — personal and cultural — on a quest to find and free her own power.

Uncompromising and all-encompassing, Pearce uncovers the archetype of the Burning Women of days gone by — Joan of Arc and the witch trials, through to the way women are burned today in cyber bullying, acid attacks, shaming and burnout, fearlessly examining the roots of Feminine power —what it is, how it has been controlled, and why it needs to be unleashed on the world during our modern Burning Times.

With contributions from leading burning women of our era: Isabel Abbott, ALisa Starkweather, Shiloh Sophia McCloud, Molly Remer, Julie Daley, Bethany Webster . . .

A must-read for all women! A life-changing book that fills the reader with a burning passion and desire for change.
Glennie Kindred, author of *Earth Wisdom*

Moon Time: harness the ever-changing energy of your menstrual cycle
by Lucy H. Pearce

Hailed as 'life-changing' by women around the world, *Moon Time* shares a fully embodied understanding of the menstrual cycle. Full of practical insight, empowering resources, creative activities and passion, this book will put women back in touch with their body's wisdom. Amazon #1 bestseller in Menstruation.

Lucy, your book is monumental. The wisdom in Moon Time sets a new course where we glimpse a future culture reshaped by honoring our womanhood journeys one woman at a time.
ALisa Starkweather, founder of the Red Tent Temple Movement

The Heroines Club: A Mother-Daughter Empowerment Circle
by Melia Keeton-Digby

The Heroines Club offers nourishing guidance and a creative approach for mothers and daughters, aged 7+, to learn and grow together through the study of women's history. Each month focuses on a different heroine, featuring athletes, inventors, artists, and revolutionaries from around the world – including Frida Kahlo, Rosalind Franklin, Amelia Earhart, Anne Frank, Maya Angelou and Malala Yousafzai as strong role models for young girls to learn about, look up to, and be inspired by.

Offering thought-provoking discussion, powerful rituals, and engaging creative activities, *The Heroines Club* fortifies our daughters' self-esteem, invigorates mothers' spirits, and nourishes the mother-daughter relationship in a culture that can make mothering daughters seem intimidating and isolating.

The Heroines Club is truly a must-have book for mothers who wish to foster a deeper connection with their daughters. As mothers, we are our daughter's first teacher, role model, and wise counsel. This book should be in every woman's hands, and passed down from generation to generation.
Wendy Cook, founder of Mighty Girl Art

The Other Side of the River:
Stories of Women, Water and the World
by Eila Kundrie Carrico

A deep searching into the ways we become dammed and how we recover fluidity. It is a journey through memory and time, personal and shared landscapes to discover the source, the flow and the deltas of women and water.

Part memoir, part manifesto, part travelogue and part love letter to myth and ecology, *The Other Side of the River* is an intricately woven tale of finding your flow . . . and your roots.

An instant classic for the new paradigm.
Lucia Chiavola Birnbaum, award-winning author
and Professor Emeritus

Reaching for the Moon: a girl's guide to her cycles
by Lucy H. Pearce

The girls' version of Lucy H. Pearce's Amazon bestselling book *Moon Time*. For girls aged 9–14, as they anticipate and experience their body's changes. *Reaching for the Moon* is a nurturing celebration of a girl's transformation to womanhood. Also available in French, Dutch and Polish editions.

A message of wonder, empowerment, magic and beauty in the shared secrets of our femininity . . . written to encourage girls to embrace their transition to womanhood in a knowledgeable, supported, loving way.

thelovingparent.com

The Heart of the Labyrinth by Nicole Schwab

Reminiscent of Paulo Coelho's masterpiece *The Alchemist* and Lynn V. Andrew's acclaimed *Medicine Woman* series, *The Heart of the Labyrinth* is a beautifully evocative spiritual parable, filled with exotic landscapes and transformational soul lessons.

Once in a while, a book comes along that kindles the fire of our inner wisdom so profoundly, the words seem to leap off the page and go straight into our heart. If you read only one book this year, this is it.

Dean Ornish, M.D., President, Preventive Medicine Research Institute, Clinical Professor of Medicine, University of California, Author of *The Spectrum*

Womancraft
PUBLISHING

Life-changing, paradigm-shifting books
by women, for women

**Visit us at
www.womancraftpublishing.com
where you can sign up to the mailing
list for discounts and samples of our
forthcoming titles before anyone else.**

(f) Womancraft Publishing

(y) WomancraftBooks

(o) Womancraft Publishing

If you have enjoyed this book, please leave
a review on Amazon or Goodreads.

Lightning Source UK Ltd.
Milton Keynes UK
UKHW040314231118
332828UK00001B/111/P